THE
MOTIVATION
HOAX

THE MOTIVATION HOAX

A SMART PERSON'S GUIDE TO INSPIRATIONAL NONSENSE

JAMES ADONIS

NERO

Published by Nero,
an imprint of Schwartz Publishing Pty Ltd
Level 1, 221 Drummond Street
Carlton VIC 3053, Australia
enquiries@blackincbooks.com
www.nerobooks.com

National Library of Australia Cataloguing-in-Publication entry:

9781760640163 (paperback)
9781743820131 (ebook)

 A catalogue record for this
book is available from the
NATIONAL
LIBRARY National Library of Australia
OF AUSTRALIA

Cover design by Peter Long
Text design and typesetting by Marilyn de Castro

Printed by Sheridan in the United States of America

CONTENTS

For my beloved Raz, a spectacular human being who probably disagrees with most of this book, but who I nonetheless cherish and adore.

INTRODUCTION

This is not an anti-motivation book. Some of the people I'm most in awe of are motivational writers and thinkers – people such as Edward Deci, William Kahn and Carol Dweck, who developed theories about self-determination, personal engagement and the growth mindset, respectively.

Nor is this an anti-quotation book. Some quotes are quite profound. I always get a kick out of the famous words of Christopher Columbus ('You can never cross the ocean until you have the courage to lose sight of the shore'), William Ward ('Feeling gratitude and not expressing it is like wrapping a present and not giving it') and the immortal W.C. Fields ('If at first you don't succeed, try, try again. Then give up. There's no use in being a damn fool about it').

Simply, this is an anti-motivational-BS book. I wrote it to counter the pervasive non-wisdom of absolutist quotations and sayings that are either fundamentally untrue or full of holes.

It's important to note, though, that the critical and perhaps even cynical approach of this book is not an attack on those whose words it discusses. The individuals I write about are invariably more successful and brilliant than me. My arguments are strictly only with particular one-off statements they made – statements that have been adopted by the motivationally privileged in ways that generalise, oversimplify or mislead, however unintentionally.

In fact I, too, am guilty of doing exactly that in the past. I've included some of these quotes (and others) in articles and books and speeches and workshops. I, too, have shared the social media posts and put up the posters and changed my laptop's wallpaper. Sometimes I've diligently followed the advice, and I've ignored it just as often. I've done all that and more, neglecting the whole time my suspicion that something about these quotations wasn't quite right. And that's because many were actually quite wrong.

That, really, is what this book is about. It's not a sanctimonious self-help guide. It's not a patronising treatise on how you can live a better life. It's just an attempt to correct the incorrect, no matter how warmly and universally it has been embraced.

1

THE INDISPUTABLE
ROLE OF LUCK

Please don't believe Ralph Waldo Emerson that **'shallow men believe in luck; strong men believe in cause and effect'**. You're not shallow at all for believing the inalienable truth that luck is at the core of a lot of cause and a lot of effect. And don't be disheartened by Thomas Jefferson when you stumble across his quip: **'I'm a greater believer in luck, and I find the harder I work the more I have of it.'** Or Samuel Goldwyn's: **'The harder I work, the luckier I get.'** You can work as hard as you can and still be stuck on a treadmill, or you can be lucky and be lifted off it by a saviour of some sort. And please ignore Serena Williams when you hear her attributing her success to matters other than luck (**'luck has nothing to do with it'**). Luck has an enormous amount to do with it – the body she was born with, the country she was raised in, the events that shaped her life, the people she met – along with many more factors that no amount of practice and sweat could make up for.

Speaking of sweat, when you see a meme that glorifies Ray Kroc, the founder of McDonald's, for stating that **'luck is a dividend of sweat; the more you sweat, the luckier you get'**, always remember there are millions of people in this world – millions and millions – who have immense wealth, stellar careers and thriving businesses without sweating at all. Why? Because they're lucky. Lucky to have been in the right place at the right time. Lucky to have thought of a killer idea while they were asleep. Lucky to be smart enough, healthy enough, safe enough, funded enough and supported enough to achieve what seems like overnight success. It is definitely not true, as Douglas MacArthur attests, that **'the best luck of all is the luck you make for yourself'**.

That's not to say that some success can't be attributed to cause and effect, or that hard work won't make you successful, or that sweating won't help you achieve your goals. Any of those things can certainly play a role. But to simply rule out luck as an influential factor – often a massively and perhaps a decisively influential factor – in your accomplishments is to have an inflated view of your skills and abilities. It is utter nonsense to think that what you have in life is only because of you and your actions.

Even Tiger Woods, arguably one of the most supremely gifted sportspeople of all time, concedes that every tournament he's won can be attributed, in part, to luck. That doesn't discount skill. It doesn't discount talent. But neither does it discount the logical conclusion that 'achievements in sport usually reflect varying degrees of skill and luck'.[1] The luck might be minor, such as the arrival of weather that creates conditions under which Woods performs more skilfully, or it might be major, such as an injury to a strong opponent.

Sport is not the only industry in which luck remains unacknowledged among the praised and hero-worshipped. The world of the corporate CEO is another. Many senior executives are praised for their strategic nous, their sound judgement, their leadership skills, their timely decisions. They're often interviewed about their tips for career success, their advice for influencing

---

1   R. Simon, 2007, 'Deserving to be lucky: Reflections on the role of luck and desert in sports', *Journal of the Philosophy of Sport*, vol. 34, no. 1, pp. 13–25.

others, their insights on managing difficult stakehold-
ers, their guidance on getting from good to great.
Rarely, however, are they written about in the context
of luck. The luck of having received a decent education.
The luck of having an encyclopaedic mind. The luck of
inheriting a booming business. The luck of being the
beneficiary of lax regulation or government incentives.
The schaudenfreudian luck of a competitor becoming
insolvent, or a monopoly being protected.

That is, of course, unless it's a question of bad luck.
In one study, over 200 managers were asked to articulate the role of luck in their organisations' success. In
the event of poor performance, they were most likely
to blame bad luck. In the event of good performance,
they were more likely to attribute the success to other
factors, such as cost minimisation, product differenti-
ation or strategic planning. In other words, to factors
they could personally influence. But here's the clincher.
In that same study, which was conducted anonymously,
the higher up the chain of command the managers were,
the more likely they were to admit that luck had played
a big role in their success.[2] In other words, the more

---

2   J.A. Parnell & E.B. Dent, 2009, 'The role of luck in the strategy-
     performance relationship', *Management Decision*, vol. 47, no. 6,
     pp. 1000–1021.

thoroughly a manager had understood their organisation, the more he or she realised how little influence they'd actually had. But hush – let's not tell anyone, because that would ruin the motivational story of the wise leader who, by dint of hard work and/or genius, led the way to corporate victory.

This is why one of the biggest analyses ever conducted on workplace luck – one that reviewed every credible study ever undertaken on the topic – reached the logical conclusion that 'exceptional performers in these contexts should not necessarily impress us because the winners are likely to have enjoyed early luck of the draw'. But when we're personally the winner, when we're the ones who have sweated and toiled and sacrificed and fought, of course we attribute our success to all that gruelling work, and of course we'll want to take the credit and the glory and the medals, all the while keeping quiet about our old friend luck, who gave us an encouraging nudge in the right direction every now and then, and occasionally a powerful shove. 'As a result, people often overestimate the role of skill and underestimate the role of luck in their counterfactual imaginations, mistaking luck for skill,' the study concludes. And so executives who usually have very little that differentiates them in terms of skill or talent end up being paid millions of dollars and rewarded with enduring fame in the business world, while their luck-less peers, often through no fault of their own, succumb to the humiliation of an ordinary wage and the feeling they have failed. 'This thus creates a mismatch: well-intended actions or competent managers are blamed for the failures outside of their control,' the study notes, 'while ill-intended actions or incompetent managers are rewarded for achievements that were outside of their control.'[3]

The authors of that study tell the fortunate story of Bill Gates, who admits that his success can be attributed to 'an incredibly lucky series of events'. He was, for example, born into a wealthy family that funded his private-school education at one of the few institutions in the 1970s to have computers, while it was his mother's useful connection to an IBM executive that enabled Gates to source funding for his start-up. Anyone who studies Gates' success in the hope that they'll be able to imitate and replicate what he achieved is at risk of barrelling towards a dead end: 'even if one could imitate everything that the most successful did, one would not be able to replicate their

3   C. Liu & M. de Rond, 2016, 'Good night, and good luck: Perspectives on luck in management scholarship', *Academy of Management Annals*, vol. 10, no. 1, pp. 409–451.

initial fortune and path dependency'.

What does this all mean? Well, it certainly doesn't imply that we should stop trying. Let's try our hardest. Nor does it mean we should assume that luck is the sole cause of all great performance. Let's still acknowledge skill and effort. We shouldn't ignore the bestsellers and how-to guides that tell us how to become just like Tiger Woods or Bill Gates. But let's also accept the humble, if dispiriting, truth that 'there are no rules for becoming the richest . . . This implies that preaching how to move from good to great is likely to lead to disappointment or even encourage excessive risk taking, fraud even, because exceptional performances are unlikely to be achieved otherwise.'

You might suspect those claims are exaggerated. They're not. In a study that compared Americans' and Europeans' perceptions of social welfare, it was found that the differences led to a number of consequences. When asked to explain why people live in poverty, 54 per cent of Europeans blamed it on bad luck, as opposed to only 30 per cent of Americans. In the United States, therefore, a vast majority of people fundamentally believe that destitution of the most extreme kind is the culpability of the individuals affected. Such a belief in luck's limitations results in decreased social spending on public health benefits, unemployment programs and pensions, thereby further entrenching social inequality.[4]

Nowhere is the presence of luck more profound than in the pursuit of music superstardom. Millions of people aspire to dominate the music industry but only a handful ever do – and they manage it not because they're the best singer or the best dancer but because they have been really, really, really lucky. This was exemplified in research that examined the albums awarded gold status by the Recording Industry Association of America over a span of decades. Some 1377 performers were represented. What the researchers found in their empirical analysis was that the success of pop stars has a lot to do with the buying behaviour of consumers. More specifically, consumers rarely have the time or inclination to conduct a thorough search of undiscovered talented singers; instead, many simply blindly purchase the records of those who are already popular, thereby making the popular even more popular and the invisible even less visible. This leads to the conclusions that 'the superstar phenomenon could exist among individuals with equal talent' (it's just that some of them are blessed with luck that helps them rise

---

4   A. Alesina, E, Glaeser & B. Sacerdote, 2001, 'Why doesn't the
     US have a European-style welfare system?', *Brookings Papers
     on Economic Activity*, vol. 3, no. 1, pp. 1–66.

above the rest), and that 'very large incomes of super-stars are driven by sheer fortune rather than by their superior (if any) talent'.[5] And let's say the success of a famous performer or athlete can somehow be entirely attributed to their supreme prowess – even that, surely, is down to the luck that comes from being born with a magnificent voice, or the luck of having been raised in a way that makes it easy for these fortunate souls to be disciplined and to prioritise the athleticism and focus that dance demands, or the luck of knowing how to instinctively write music that makes hearts sing, or the luck that comes with not having endured a career-killing injury.

Just once, at an awards show, it would be nice for a recipient to acknowledge the truth. How lovely, how refreshing would it be for a Hall of Fame inductee to simply admit: 'I was lucky. Yes, I worked hard; yes, I had a supportive partner; yes, I thank God and my fans and my producer; but more than anyone, more than anything, I would like to thank Lady Luck, because there are millions of people on this planet who are more talented than me, have worked harder

5   K.H. Chung & R.A.K. Cox, 1994, 'A stochastic model of super-stardom: An application of the Yule distribution', *The Review of Economics and Statistics*, vol. 76, no. 4, pp. 771–775.

than me, have greater self-belief than me, have taken more risks than me, and yet I'm the one standing here receiving this prestigious award. So, Lady Luck, I thank you.'

It is for that simple reason – that even the best aren't really, seriously the actual best – that the scholars can conclude that 'one should not imitate the highest performers nor dismiss the worst performers' – because the worst may not be the worst because they're crappy, but rather because they're unlucky. The aforementioned scholars demonstrated that particular effect in a simulation they designed, which included the computational analysis of 5 million players competing for the highest number of manufactured successes in a game. They compared the players who were able to win 40 rounds with those who could win 50. It's true that skill played a vital role among those who got to 40. But the difference among those who made it to 50 had nothing at all to do with skill. In fact, those who got to 50 actually had a lower level of skill than those who got to 40. 'Stated differently, the most successful players are not the most impressive,' the study concluded. They were just the luckiest. More elaborately, 'an extreme performance indicates that it was achieved in a context in which chance events can substantially influence outcomes, and performance is then an unreliable indicator of skill'.[6]

One final example, this time in relation to wealth; more specifically, to stock market wealth. 'Modern western mythology is filled with success stories, in which the poor but ambitious and talented hero becomes a millionaire,' writes scholar S.M. Levy. He goes on to say that 'there are two competing explanations for the uneven distribution of wealth in society': one is talent; the other is luck. We already know it's a mixture of both, but which of the two is dominant? Levy analysed the wealthiest people in the United States, focusing on how they made their investment decisions (since investment income is the source from which they derived most of their wealth). What he discovered was that they each held similar return distributions, which means they didn't differ much in talent, because if talent were the sole predictor of their success, there'd be significantly greater variance in their returns. Therefore, 'the main factor responsible for the uneven distribution of wealth at the high wealth range is pure chance'. Investment knowhow is important, but only up to a certain point. Beyond that, 'it is only luck that differentiates' the haves

---

6   J. Denrell & C. Liu, 2012, 'Top performers are not the most impressive when extreme performance indicates unreliability', *Proceedings of the National Academy of Sciences*, vol. 109, no. 24, pp. 9331–9336.

from the also-haves-but-not-to-the-same-obscene-extent. 'Those who are most successful owe it primarily to their luck, and not to abnormal investment abilities,' Levy concludes.[7]

So let's modify, then, the quotations that began this chapter so that they more accurately reflect reality:

Ralph Waldo Emerson:

> **'Grateful people believe in luck. Conceited people believe only in cause and effect.'**

Thomas Jefferson:

> **'I'm a greater believer in luck, and I find the harder I work the more I can leverage it, should I be fortunate enough for it to come my way.'**

Samuel Goldwyn:

> **'The harder I work, the luckier I get – and that is almost certainly correlation, not causation.'**

---

7   S.M. Levy, 2003, 'Are rich people smarter?', *Journal of Economic Theory*, vol. 110, no. 1, pp. 42–64.

Serena Williams:

> **'Luck has almost everything to do with it.'**

Ray Kroc:

> **'The more you eat McDonald's,
> the unluckier you get.'**[8]

Douglas MacArthur:

> **'The best luck of all is the lottery.'**

---

8 As evidenced by M. Spurlock, 2004, *Super Size Me*, Roadside
Attractions, Samuel Goldwyn Films, Showtime Independent Films.

2

'A QUITTER NEVER WINS AND A WINNER NEVER QUITS'

—NAPOLEON HILL

This notable quotation praises staying power. But its categorical assumption that one must never quit unless one wants to win is dangerous insofar that, sometimes – perhaps often – the key to winning is the preparedness to acknowledge that occasionally it's time to bow out.

Indeed, to persist can actually be counterproductive. In one experiment,[9] participants were given 60 seconds to respond to each task-related item. Some were easy,

---

9   D.B. McFarlin, R.F. Baumeister & K. Blascovich, 1984, 'On knowing when to quit: Task failure, self-esteem, advice, and nonproductive persistence', *Journal of Personality*, vol. 52, no. 2, pp. 138–155.

others hard. The participants themselves were grouped into those who had high rates of self-esteem and those whose self-esteem was low. The results showed that those with high self-esteem were actually less productive than their counterparts. Here's why.

Those with high self-esteem stuck with the difficult problems longer. They continued working on them, desperately trying to figure out the right answer. By contrast, those with low self-esteem usually skipped the tough questions. This meant they could progress through the experiment at a faster rate, thereby answering more of the easier questions – so that by the end of the experiment they had outperformed their more confident peers.

The scholars concluded: 'The tendency for individuals with high expectations (high self-esteem) to continue to persist, especially after failure, may sometimes prove maladaptive. High self-esteem subjects' apparent refusal to give up ... especially after failure ... resulted in non-productive persistence and poorer performance relative to low self-esteem subjects.'

According to the researchers, the implications of this experiment extends beyond the laboratory. Life is full of examples where failure may be a good reason to give up rather than persevere. To continue unabated without a harsh reality check can at times result in further failures, many of which might prove costly – both financially and emotionally. They list three specific examples:

- *Warfare:* Continuing the same military strategy in the face of repeated defeat will likely only bring further casualties.

- *Sport:* Adopting the same manoeuvre may eventually generate a win, but it may be more effective to try different moves.

- *Science:* Repeated rejections by journal publishers may indicate that the continuous resubmission of a paper might be less effective than rewriting the paper or changing the methodology.

So what's the antidote? It's something known as 'rational optimisation', which means that when confronted by failure, we shouldn't automatically think the next best step is to do the same thing with greater effort. Instead, we ought to pause and reflect on the worthiness of the goal, the effectiveness of the technique, and whether our approach for the next attempt (if another attempt is required at all) should change either a little or a lot.

The tendency to persevere despite a mountain of opposing evidence can be seen particularly in the field of inventions. Inventors, who tend to be more optimistic and confident than the rest of us, passionately develop their new gadgets in the hope they'll change the world – or their own bank balances. Irrespective of the motivation, how they react to repeated failure, and the consequences that then ensue, would surely make for a fascinating study.

Which, thankfully, has already been done. In an analysis of 756 Canadian inventors,[10] researchers looked at those who were advised to give up because the indicators for success were discouraging. By and large, those who were told to give up tended to heed the advice. They wisely called it quits. Others persevered. And I guess if you looked closely enough at those who persevered despite the advice to give up, you might find one or two who went on to achieve massive success – and who now proselytise about the importance of not listening to detractors and the need to follow your dreams no matter what anyone says. But to

---

10   T. Astebro, S.A. Jeffrey & G.K. Adomdza, 2007, 'Inventor perseverance after being told to quit: the role of cognitive biases', *Journal of Behavioral Decision Making*, vol. 20, no. 3, pp. 253–272.

look at those one or two outliers as a reason to keep going when objective experts are telling you to change course . . . well, that just doesn't make sense. Because what ended up happening in this study is that those deluded dream-followers (I'm not using the word 'deluded' in a derogatory fashion; it just denotes those whose optimism is somewhat misdirected) ended up experiencing a range of adverse outcomes.

One clearly adverse outcome was financial. When extremely optimistic inventors were compared to moderately optimistic inventors, the extremely optimistic continued to spend money even when being advised to stop. How much more did they spend? Approximately 166 per cent more than the others. Another variable was in relation to experience. When inventors with more than three years' experience were compared to inventors with fewer than three years' experience, the more experienced inventors went on to spend 301 per cent more on their inventions despite being told to quit. Money aside, they also spent 175 per cent more time on their projects, even though the evidence indicated they'd be better off trying something else.

What this finding demonstrates is that inventors who had invested significant money and time before receiving negative advice were far more likely to continue pursuing their dreams, thereby wasting even more money and even more time. A majority would have been better off cutting their losses and redirecting their funds and energy to more promising endeavours. The researchers sum it up succinctly: 'Those who receive advice to stop should be spending no additional resources . . . While optimism can be healthy for the psyche, it may lead people to spend money on losing propositions.'

Driving this behaviour is a perilous condition commonly referred to as 'egotistical illusion'. An egotistical illusion occurs when individuals have inflated views of themselves. This isn't to suggest at all that self-esteem is a bad thing. It's obviously positive, beneficial and necessary. But we're not talking about ordinary self-esteem here. What we're talking about is self-esteem to the power of ten. It's a view of one's self so unrealistic that it culminates in the setting of goals that aren't just overly ambitious, they're downright impossible to achieve. This excessive self-belief doesn't give people power; it weakens them. It makes them more vulnerable, especially because, when faced with failure, they're too blinded by their own sense of superiority to realise that the failure is not an obstacle to overcome but a reason to stop, take a deep breath and reflect. In truth, failure can be a warning rather than an obstruction.

In a series of interesting experiments,[11] egotistical illusionists were found to 'perform more aggressively than usual, presumably out of a desire to achieve an impressive success, but the increase in speed brought a loss of accuracy, and the result was counterproductive'. Let's look at the three experiments more closely.

In the first, participants were asked to play a video game – one of those simple tasks where they were required to navigate a plane while trying to avoid targets such as trees and hot-air balloons. Whenever they bumped into an object, they crashed, thereby wasting valuable time. Some participants were also told that they could set their own more ambitious goals, the achievement of which would result in the generation of real prize money. The egotistical illusionists, obsessed with achieving superior performance, increased their plane's speed at the sacrifice of accuracy. Their planes frequently crashed. So, too, did they.

The second experiment upped the ante. This time, participants were given money in advance and were told they could bet it on themselves. By making a minimal

---

11   R.F. Baumeister, T.F. Heatherton & D.M. Tice, 1993, 'When ego threats lead to self-regulation failure: Negative consequences of high self-esteem', *Journal of Personality and Social Psychology*, vol. 64, no. 1, pp. 141–156.

bet, the participants were able to keep the money they were given. But by making an audacious bet, they were creating the opportunity to leave with much more – but also with much less. So who do you think were most likely to bet on themselves the most aggressively? Yep, the egotistical illusionists. And who were the most likely to lose? Again, the egotistical illusionists, many of whom bet and lost everything they had.

The third experiment was broadly the same as the other two, but with one notable change worth mentioning. At the end of the study, the egotistical illusionists were asked to describe how they felt. As might be expected, betting big and losing it all resulted in feelings of distress, anger, disappointment, frustration, embarrassment and regret. Their high self-esteem no longer acted as a buffer against the adverse effects of extending themselves.

In their conclusion, the researchers hypothetically propose that two people who have the same level of ability and equally high self-esteem might be differentiated by the extent to which they set their goals. The one not afflicted by egotistical illusions is the one more likely to be prudent when determining performance objectives, and therefore has a greater likelihood of success. The other's prospects are far less encouraging. As the scholars note, it is these egotistical illusionists who become preoccupied with trying to save face and to make a good impression. Their self-esteem could have been preserved had they set realistic goals – in other words, had they known when to quit.

With this in mind, here is a more accurate version of Napoleon Hill's quotation:

'A quitter can win and a winner can quit.'

3

PASSION: A TALE OF DESTRUCTIVE OBSESSION

Most of us have at least one passion – an activity, a mission, an exercise, an art, a food, a country, an animal, a person – the existence of which is a core part of what excites us in life. So long as it remains a harmonious passion. This goes against what many of the world's most successful people encourage us to do. It's easy for folk like Facebook's Sheryl Sandberg to state **'it is the ultimate luxury to combine passion and contribution. It's also a very clear path to happiness'**. (It's actually not, but more on that later.) Likewise, when theologian John Wesley urged his followers to **'light yourself on fire with passion and people will come from**

miles to watch you burn', it's quite possible his disciples' red-hot glow was an incandescent rage sparked
by futility and exasperation. Even humanitarian busi-
nesswoman Anita Roddick's advice that **'to succeed
you have to believe in something with such a passion
that it becomes reality'** – well, many of the world's
most successful individuals are really only passionate
about success. The means of getting there has more to
do with calculated risk, meticulous strategy and, as we
now know, a truckload of luck – plus, as we'll discuss in
a later chapter, many unfair advantages. Celebrity chef
Julia Child probably had no idea that telling people to
**'find something you're passionate about and keep
tremendously interested in it'** can actually be tremendously perilous, as we'll soon discover.

Credit for exposing the dark side of passion belongs
to a group of Canadian researchers, who in 2003 empirically delineated two types of passion: harmonious and
obsessive. The former is a mild and gratifying variety
that can generate motivation and fulfilment, while the
latter is destined to 'arouse negative emotions, lead to
inflexible persistence, and interfere with achieving a
balanced, successful life'. This is apt when you consider
the etymology of the word 'passion': *passio* is Latin for
suffering. The academics noted that 'individuals with
a passion are seen as passive, as slaves to their passion.

Their passion controls them.'[12]

Now, you might think the distinction between harmonious passion and obsessive passion is obvious, thereby rendering the quotations in the opening paragraph of this chapter correct. But as you'll see from the following statements, which the researchers identified in their study as being reflective of obsessive passion, it becomes apparent these obsessive passions are very much like everyday passions:

- I cannot live without [the passion].

- The urge is so strong I can't help myself from doing this activity.

- My mood depends on me being able to do this activity.

We're talking here about run-of-the-mill passions like dance, sport, reading and playing musical instruments, but each of those statements clearly evinced the

12   R.J. Vallerand, C. Blanchard, G.A. Mageau, R. Koestner, C. Ratelle, M. Leonard, M. Gagne & J. Marsolais, 2003, 'Les passions de l'ame: On obsessive and harmonious passion', *Journal of Personality and Social Psychology*, vol. 85, no. 4, pp. 756–767.

burning sensation that John Wesley preached, as well as the 'tremendous' incitements of Julia Child.

An example of the adverse consequences of passion can be found in sport – more specifically, in the aggression that often adheres to sport. Not just among players but among fans too, and even among parents at their kids' games. Why is that? Because of obsessive passion.

But what is it specifically about obsessive passion that can often make its slaves so aggressive? To find out, the researchers tested more than 200 basketball players in a number of different studies, and asked them if they could respond in the affirmative to statements like this: 'At times I cannot control my urge to harm an opponent.' Those who said yes were, unsurprisingly, more likely to be driven by obsessive passion, and the reason it morphed into aggression is because the moment someone becomes obsessively passionate, they immediately associate that passion with their self-identity. They become their passion, and their passion becomes them. Any threat to their passion is a threat to them personally. Similarly, any criticism, mistake or failure is not just an attack on what they hold dear, but an attack on who they are as a person. 'It is thus not surprising that these athletes are willing to do almost anything to preserve their identity as competent basketball players, including injuring other players who pose a threat to this crucial aspect of their identity,' write the scholars.[13]

Some people might say that even though unfortunate consequences exist, obsessive passion is nonetheless what generates results. It's the key to goal achievement! The path to success! Or, to quote Sheryl Sandberg, it's how to be happy! If only. Because then it'd make all the effort and sacrifice worth it.

The disconnect between happiness and obsessive passion was demonstrated in another study, this time on 143 dramatic arts students who had been accepted into a highly competitive and elite school.[14] What they discovered was that both harmonious passion (the mild and pleasant variety) and obsessive passion compelled the students to practise more vigorously and dedicatedly, and that this improved their performance. However, those who were obsessively passionate responded negatively to questions about their general satisfaction in life. These findings were replicated in a second study, this time on 130 psychology students who had been

---

13   E.G. Donahue, B. Rip, & R.J. Vallerand, 2009, 'When winning is everything: On passion, identity, and aggression in sport', *Psychology of Sport and Exercise*, vol. 10, no. 5, pp. 526–534.

14   R.J. Vallerand, S.J. Salvy, G.A. Mageau, A.J. Elliot, P.L. Denis, F.M.E. Grouzet & C. Blanchard, 2007, 'On the role of passion in performance', *Journal of Personality*, vol. 75, no. 3, pp. 505–534.

accepted to a psychology course that had an 85 per cent rejection rate. These highly gifted and passionate students were then tested on their passion type and their final grades. As expected, those who were obsessively passionate were miserable about life in comparison to their peers. This can perhaps be explained by what motivates the two groups. Whereas harmoniously passionate people are driven by a sense of fulfilment, mastery and achievement in the task itself, the obsessively passionate are also compelled by an intense need to avoid failure, to avoid looking incompetent and to outdo others. This means they're conflicted: one part of them strives for success because they want to master their craft, while the other part of them is engaging in maladaptive motivators and behaviours that can 'have a deleterious influence on performance'. So not only are they less happy, they're also subsequently less successful than they would have been if they had toned the passion down. The researchers conclude: 'It would thus appear that the popular image of obsessively passionate performers who focus exclusively on their activity at the expense of other aspects of their lives, and who end up achieving high levels of performance, may only represent a part of the picture.'

The other part, as we now know, is unappealing. And it's a phenomenon that's replicated in the workplace.

Let's look at one place of work in particular where passions are not uncommonly brought to the fore: the hospital. More specifically, among nurses working within the hospital.

Imagine the existence of two nurses, Judy and Jim. They're both passionate about their work. There are, however, some key distinctions:

- For Judy, nursing is the one core passion in her life. She can't imagine living without it. She can't stop thinking about it and talking about it. Her patients, her colleagues and her place of work occupy her thoughts even when she's not at work. Judy is clearly obsessively passionate.

- For Jim, nursing is one of several passions. This means that when he leaves work, other interests engage him, such as family and various hobbies. He enjoys his work and does his best, but it doesn't consume him. Jim is harmoniously passionate.

These characterisations and their ensuing consequences were explored by researchers investigating whether the two types of passion affect passionistas in differing ways in the professional arena. They conducted two studies. In the first, nurses were asked to state the extent to which they could relate to statements such as 'I have difficulties controlling my urge to do my work'. As can be expected, these nurses were significantly more likely to be burnt out because of the detrimental impact that such dedication to their work had on their personal lives. The second study was almost identical, except that this time the nurses – 258 of them, in Canada – were surveyed twice, six months apart. Such longitudinal research is extremely valuable because the enduring nature of findings further validates the data. Well, the results remained the same. Even over the longer term, work/life conflict and burnout emerged as bedfellows of the obsessively passionate, even when that passion was directed into important areas such as nursing, a job that genuinely helps people and makes the world a better place. And yet, even then, there's little saving those who are doing the saving.

The researchers summarise their conclusions as follows: 'The type of passion that one has for an activity that he or she engages in on a regular basis (such as work) matters greatly with respect to burnout.' But here, in my opinion, is the most vital part of what they discovered: even high rates of work satisfaction are not enough to protect passionistas from these adverse effects: 'it would appear that one's rigid engagement toward one's work induced by obsessive passion prevents one from experiencing any work satisfaction and, on top of that, leads to conflict between work and other life activities.'[15]

One final study – there are dozens and dozens of these, by the way – before we move on. Like me, these researchers were fascinated by the reams of findings disproving the supposed benefits of obsessive passion, despite those in the motivational press who promote it as an essential ingredient of success. Obsessive passion, for example, has been found to result in feelings of resentment towards the object about which an individual was once passionate. It's also a form of passion that's been found to lead to addiction, pathological behaviour, interpersonal conflict and dependency.

And now yet another consequence can be added to the list. Scholars focused on dancers, who have previously been empirically identified as being more perfectionistic, neurotic and anxious than those who work in many other professions. This is perhaps a consequence of the hyper-competitive and ruthlessly critical world in which they operate. Anyway, the researchers assessed 100 dancers, half of them male and half female, from a diversity of styles, such as jazz, hip-hop, modern and ballet.

---

15   R.J. Vallerand, Y. Paquet, F.L. Philippe & J. Charest, 2010, 'On the role of passion for work in burnout: a process model', *Journal of Personality*, vol. 78, no. 1, pp. 289–312.

The dancers were given statements with which to agree or disagree, including 'I feel anxious if I cannot dance', 'I am unable to reduce how often I dance' and 'my dance [interferes] with family responsibilities'. Unsurprisingly, those who were obsessively passionate were found to agree strongly with those statements. They were also more likely to then engage in a range of risky behaviours, such as avoiding visits to the doctor even when handicapped by an injury of some sort.[16]

We can fairly conclude, then, that the quotations that began this chapter need to be reworked, starting with Sheryl Sandberg:

> **'It is the ultimate luxury to combine passion and contribution. It can also be a very clear path to unhappiness.'**

John Wesley:

> **'Light yourself on fire with passion and people will come from miles to watch you burn. Perhaps literally.'**

---

16   S.A. Akehurst & E.J. Oliver, 2014, 'Obsessive passion: a dependency associated with injury-related risky behaviour in dancers', *Journal of Sports Sciences*, vol. 32, no. 3, pp. 259–267.

Anita Roddick:

> 'To succeed you have to believe in something with only just enough passion that it becomes reality.'

Julia Child:

> 'Find something you're passionate about and keep harmoniously interested in it.'

4

'CHOOSE A JOB YOU LOVE, AND YOU WILL NEVER HAVE TO WORK A DAY IN YOUR LIFE'

—CONFUCIUS

Let's put aside the first word of this enduring Confucian wisdom and focus instead on the core essence of its inaccuracy: the notion that a lovable job does not equate to hard work – or work at all, for that matter.

Actually, no, it would be remiss of us to overlook that first word, since it represents much of what's wrong with this quotation. That word – *choose* – claims that people really do have a choice when selecting their job. It insinuates that those of us in jobs we hate, or jobs we mildly dislike, have intentionally chosen those career paths. One might even say that to be spoiled for career choice is a luxury of living in the West – which would be amusing, considering the origin of this quotation. Even among those living in the First World, though, a vast majority have little choice in the vocation they end up pursuing. It's usually a selection between Ordinary, Crap and Shit – and sometimes just Crap and Shit. For reasons of poverty, lack of opportunity, limited intellect and other forms of non-self-inflicted disadvantage, the freedom to choose one's career so that it generates this thing called 'love' is really only in the purview of the few.

It's nice to imagine that choice is widely available – that we can choose to be a ballerina or a sports star, a carpenter or a writer, a teacher or a fashion designer – but the sad reality is we cannot. Most people are stuck with choosing between cleaning homes or cleaning offices, working in factories or working in call centres, driving cabs or driving trucks. The sort of choice to which Confucius referred has, more often than not, been unavailable to many workers. In many cases, the only choice they have is between working and not working at all.

But anyway. Let's move on to the core issue, which is essentially the notion that a job you love is the ticket you need to a life in which work doesn't really exact a toll. In order to articulate the inaccuracy of this quotation, it's important to explain a term known as 'employee engagement', which is a better way to conceive of the 'love' an individual might feel at work.

Employee engagement occurs when an employee is so switched on at work – so motivated, focused, interested and involved – they end up producing some of the best work imaginable for their employer. Engaged employees are almost always connected meaningfully to their organisation on three different levels: (i) they exert greater physical effort in the work they do; (ii) they invest more of their cognitive capacity into their tasks; and (iii) they feel emotionally linked to their boss, their colleagues, their employer and, yes, their job. So when we talk about choosing a job you really love, the only construct we should be looking at is employee engagement, because it represents the most deeply infatuated of workplace-related loves. Which means that if you're a devotee of Confucius's quotation, you might assume you wouldn't necessarily be 'working' if you happened to be engaged at work. But this isn't true. For various reasons.

Let's begin with what's perhaps the most obvious: that no one actually loves their job all of the time. No job is ever that perfect. This means that even the best and most lovable of jobs will contain experiences you absolutely love and experiences you seriously loathe. And as the most credible of research tells us, this usually happens not just once in a while but every day, perhaps from hour to hour or even minute to minute.

That's why diary studies are especially instructive when we're seeking to understand the fluctuating nature of employee engagement. Since engagement is a relatively recent addition to the management lexicon, only about two dozen studies have been conducted in relation to the way it fluctuates throughout the workday. And a summary of these studies has concluded that it 'fluctuates significantly'.[17] There are many reasons why. Sometimes, employees may have a lot of support from their colleagues; other times not at all. At one moment they might have a sense they're adequately balancing work and life; at other moments they might feel it's all getting out of control. At certain points during the day, their leader might be caring and attentive, while at other times that same leader may be neglectful and inconsiderate. There are dozens of other factors that could also trigger states of engagement or disengagement.

The main thing, though, is this: even the most engaged employees experience periods of disengagement, during which the job they love is still very much,

---

17   A.B. Bakker, 2014, 'Daily fluctuations in work engagement:
      An overview and current directions', *European Psychologist*,
      vol. 19, no. 4, pp. 227–236.

well, a job. They are hit by the realisation that this is indeed work, no matter how much they try to disguise it with rhetoric that pretends it's something else.

Teachers may love their job while teaching students in the classroom, but hate it when taking them out on a school excursion. Nurses may love their job when helping patients heal, but hate it when a task results in the infliction of pain. Farmers may love their job when the harvest is bountiful, but hate it when there's drought. And these examples are merely bivariate. There are many more variables in every profession that are responsible for a large number of associated fluctuations.

Let's say, by some miracle, an employee is able to maintain a constant high level of engagement throughout the day, or that, even more generously, an employee's job can be considered a labour of 'love', so long as a majority of the day is spent in a state of engagement. Even then, it's still work.

In one particularly impressive piece of scholarly commentary,[18] employee engagement was critiqued from the perspective that almost all of the research to date has focused on the positive outcomes of engagement – for

---

18   J.M. George, 2011, 'The wider context, costs, and benefits of work engagement', *European Journal of Work and Organizational Psychology*, vol. 20, no. 1, pp. 53–59.

organisations and, to a lesser extent, employees. This research downplays 'the fact that work is a necessity for the vast majority of workers', and that 'few people would continue on their jobs, even if they were not economically dependent on them, if they were not paid'. In other words, regardless of how much people love their work, in nearly every case they would not continue if it weren't for the money hitting their bank accounts on a regular basis.

The scholar adds that 'in an era of increasing work hours and pressures, and when employees are increasingly being bombarded with work e-mails they need to respond to in the evenings, on weekends, and while on holiday, increasing levels of work engagement would certainly seem to exacerbate the feelings of overwork, stress, and work–nonwork conflict'.

Here's what that means. Employees with high rates of engagement are more committed to their work. This enhanced level of commitment frequently results in extra hours and extra grunt, the culmination of which may lead to exhaustion and an intrusion in their personal lives. They still love their work, sure, but they are indeed still working: 'Sometimes high engagement is not fun or positive and, under certain conditions, people who are disengaged might actually feel better personally than those who are highly engaged.'

This was emphasised by one of the most influential analyses on employee engagement, which concluded that 'there are limits on the pool of energy and resources available to employees'.[19] This means 'sustained levels of engagement will be difficult to achieve', because to be engaged at work requires effort. A lot of effort. Sure, it's voluntary effort, and engagement is overall a pleasant experience, but continuously investing high levels of physical, cognitive and emotional effort eventually has a physical, cognitive and emotional cost, unless there are periods of recovery from what is, at the end of the day, work, no matter how we spin it.

Even the professor who pioneered the study of employee engagement noted that to be engaged in one's work necessitates the use of emotional labour that's rarely present when one is disengaged.[20] Engagement is therefore 'relatively exhausting in terms of the vigilance and personal effort it requires . . . Nor is [engagement] always advisable. There are types of situations and organizations in which people who are [engaged] are

19   W.H. Macey & B. Schneider, 2008, 'The meaning of employee engagement', *Industrial and Organizational Psychology*, vol. 1, no. 1, pp. 3–30.

20   W.A. Kahn, 1990, 'Psychological conditions of personal engagement and disengagement at work', *The Academy of Management Journal*, vol. 33, no. 4, pp. 692–724.

exposed to the dangers of being drained with little given in return. This is the classic scenario of job burnout.'[21]

And so we come back to the old Confucian quotation, which, while well intentioned, is evidently mistaken. It might be more aptly reworded as:

'Have a job you love, and you will still have to work most days in your life.'

---

21 W.A. Kahn, 1992, 'To be fully there: Psychological presence at work', *Human Relations*, vol. 45, no. 4, pp. 321–329.

5

MONEY AND HAPPINESS: A MEDLEY OF MISLEADING QUOTATIONS

S ome kernels of motivational wisdom are graced with a multitude of likeminded quotes, probably none more so than the iniquitous marriage of money and happiness. The most emphatic quote is that of Benjamin Franklin, one of the Founding Fathers of the United States, who fathered this pronouncement: **'Money never made a man happy yet, nor will it. There is nothing in its nature to produce happiness. The more a man has, the more he wants. Instead of filling a vacuum, it makes one.'** Fast-forward more than a century, and one of his successor presidents, Franklin D. Roosevelt, cautioned: **'Happiness is not in the mere possession of money;**

it lies in the joy of achievement, in the thrill of creative effort.' And yet that thrill continued to plague people decades later, which is why motivational superstar Zig Ziglar urged his devotees that **'Money won't make you happy . . . But everybody wants to find out for themselves.'** Even Agatha Christie, the bestselling author of all time, spent some time pondering the following question while enjoying the royalties she garnered from the 2 billion books she sold: **'What good is money if it can't buy happiness?'** In contrast to the others, at least Madame Christie articulated her thoughts in the form of a question, leaving open the slim possibility – by using the qualifying word *if* – that money can indeed lead to happiness.

Well, money definitely can lead to happiness. And it is the reams of previous research demonstrating that specific relationship that led two psychologists to identify precisely how and why it happens.[22] This research concluded that money provides people with opportunities they previously did not have, which enables them to have happy experiences they otherwise wouldn't. It also concluded that when your income is low and

---

22 W. Johnson & R.F. Krueger, 2006, 'How money buys happiness: genetic and environmental processes linking finances and life satisfaction', *Journal of Personality and Social Psychology*, vol. 90, no. 4, pp. 680–691.

you're stressed every day, constantly preoccupied by money-related concerns – how to pay the bills, how to make the rent, how to give your kids the bare essentials – the patronising notion that money won't make you at least a little bit happier is so ludicrous as to be insulting. This research noted the comfort that comes from being asset-rich, because it can be a source of additional life-enriching resources.

So we can probably end this chapter right here, because there's enough evidence already to disprove the well-intentioned urgings of Franklin, Roosevelt, Ziglar and Christie. But let's continue anyway and look at a selection of fascinating studies that explore not just the connection between money and happiness, but also the mechanisms through which that connection is fortified.

Let's begin with the researchers mentioned earlier, who discovered that financial resources are 'significantly associated with life satisfaction', but noted that the phenomenon is driven strongly by the perception of one's own financial wellness. Here's what that means. Let's say you and I each have $50,000. This might make you feel really good about life and about yourself. I, in contrast, might feel dissatisfied and worthless. The difference, according to the scholars, comes down to whether you perceive $50,000 to be enough in terms of your ability to control your expenditure. The more control you think you have, the happier you'll be. A rising income enables you to cultivate more control.

What the researchers also found was that having a stash of cash provides people with a buffer that protects them from unfortunate events. The scholars use the example of a car accident that affects someone who's wealthy and someone who's poor. Assuming it's an injury-free prang, the wealthy individual can afford to get the car fixed or replaced, thereby preserving her ability to remain happy (barring the short-term inconvenience of being without a car). The poor individual, by comparison, might be psychologically tormented. He could be unable to fix or replace the car, the absence of which might affect his ability to work or to meet his family obligations.

Now, that study was microeconomic. It focused very much on individual wealth and the associated perceptions of that wealth. But from a macroeconomic perspective, too, the link between money and happiness is evident.

This was demonstrated profoundly by academics from Harvard, the London School of Economics and the University of Warwick.[23] In their analysis of hundreds

---

23   R. Di Tella, R.J. MacCulloch & A.J. Oswald, 2003, 'The macro-economics of happiness', *Review of Economics and Statistics*, vol. 85, no. 4, pp. 809–827.

of thousands of individuals from around the world, a number of intriguing and important correlations were identified. First, a nation's gross domestic product (or GDP) has a direct effect on the happiness of its citizens. More specifically, for every $1000 increase in a nation's GDP, there is a shift in happiness of 3.6 percentage points per person, leading to the conclusion that 'contemporaneous happiness and GDP are strongly correlated'.

The second result pertains to the opposite of GDP growth: a dreaded recession. Recessions, as everyone knows and fears, are associated with unemployment, bankruptcies and despair. Surely, then, we don't need a study to prove that a recession – which is, in effect, a reduction of wealth – must have a consequently negative impact on happiness. And yet that is what these esteemed scholars sought to prove. What they discovered, perhaps unsurprisingly, was that happiness is certainly impacted – not only among the unemployed but also among those who still have jobs. That's because even those who are still employed during a recession become fearful that they might be next in line to lose their jobs. That predominant fear, of course, crushes happiness.

The third finding relates to welfare. If money didn't lead to some sort of happiness, surely welfare would have a similarly negligible effect, right? Not quite.

The scholars found that the more generous the welfare state, particularly in the form of unemployment benefits, the happier a society became. The researchers concluded that 'macroeconomics matters' because of its 'strong effects on the happiness of nations'.

Let's move back to microeconomics, and a wish that many of us – probably all of us – have made at some stage: to receive a windfall of cash. If you've ever dreamed of winning the lottery, I'm possibly already preaching to the converted. The mere act of desiring such a massive windfall is associated with the hope that what it enables you to buy will also bring with it a bag or two of happiness. That's precisely what researchers found when they investigated the lives of 9000 randomly selected people.[24] Their study compared those who had received a windfall in the preceding year – such as a lottery win or an inheritance – with those who had not. Their conclusion? 'Money does buy greater happiness and lower measured stress.'

How much, exactly? Well, being the beneficiary of, say, £50,000 (which equates to approximately US$75,000

---

24   J. Gardner & A. Oswald, 2001, 'Does money buy happiness?
     A longitudinal study using data on windfalls', *Warwick University*,
     March 2001, viewed 25 June 2016, www2.warwick.ac.uk/fac/soc/
     economics/staff/ajoswald/marchwindfallsgo.pdf.

and AU$100,000) results in a rise in mental wellbeing of between 0.1 and 0.3 standard deviations. If, like me, you're not statistically minded, that might not sound like a lot – but actually it is. To put it in perspective, it means that all you'd need to move from the bottom of the happiness scale to the top is roughly £1 million. How long you'd stay there is anyone's guess, but the point to note is this: money brings happiness even if it's just temporary. And if it's only temporary, so what? Surely that's better than no lift in happiness at all? Just ask the citizens formerly known as East Germans.

In the decade following the fall of the Berlin Wall, the average household income of East Germans increased by approximately 60 per cent. Did such a significant rise in wealth also result in a rise in happiness? That's what a group of Australian scholars wanted to find out.[25] They studied tens of thousands of East Germans – and, for the purpose of comparison, West Germans too. One question was at the heart of their analysis: 'How satisfied are you at present with your life, all things considered?' The respondents rated their satisfaction between 0 and 10.

---

25   P. Frijters, J.P Haisken DeNew & M.A. Shields, 2004, 'Money does matter! Evidence from increasing real income and life satisfaction in East Germany following reunification', *American Economic Review*, vol. 94, no. 3, pp. 730–740.

The findings showed that, during the period of the analysis, while incomes in East Germany increased substantially, 'average life satisfaction in East Germany also increased considerably, while West Germans experienced a fall in life satisfaction'.

Now, one could argue that the real reason for the rise in happiness could be attributed to the newfound freedom the East Germans were suddenly enjoying, the mobility they were relishing, the better housing they were receiving, and the many public services they were being granted. And yes, those factors had a large effect, amounting to a total of about 60 per cent. But that's all of those factors *combined*. One single factor – the rise in real household income – constituted the rest. What that means is that 40 per cent of the increase in happiness that East Germans felt in the decade following reunification was due to the money that was accumulating in their bank accounts.

Let's now revise the quotations that began this chapter.

Benjamin Franklin's statement would be closer to the truth when worded like this:

'Money has made people happy, and will continue to do so. There is much in its nature

**to produce happiness. The more one has, the
more one wants. Instead of filling a vacuum,
it fills a bank balance.'**

Next in line for a revision is Franklin D. Roosevelt, who at least leaves room for the idea that the generation of money in its own right can be quite fulfilling – or, in motivational parlance, a fulfilling *journey*:

**'Happiness is in the mere possession of
money and also in the joy of achievement,
in the thrill of creative effort.'**

Zig Ziglar, too, is up for a touch-up:

**'Money can make you happy . . .
But everybody wants to find out for
themselves, which is fair enough.'**

Lastly, a modest addendum to Agatha Christie's contemplation:

**'What good is money if it can't buy
happiness? And how good is money if it can!'**

'<INSERT NOUN>
IS A JOURNEY,
NOT A DESTINATION'

Many a noun has been the focus of this ubiquitous quotation. Success. Love. Education. Happiness. Fitness. Innovation. Freedom. Quality. Digital transformation. Inbound marketing. Christian life. For the purpose of this chapter, and the avoidance of yawning as either a journey or a destination, let's limit our focus to the first three.

'Success is a journey, not a destination.'

When Deepak Chopra used this line in his book *The Seven Spiritual Laws of Success*, he took care to note that success is dependent on the way it is defined, which is rather convenient. Success, for instance, could be 'the abundant flow of all good things'. Success could also be the act of being 'in harmony with nature'. And even 'energy and enthusiasm for life'. All of those, really, are so wide-ranging as to basically equate success with the mere act of breathing, which many of us generally accept is barely a successful endeavour. Or maybe not.

'Success', as defined by the esteemed *Oxford English Dictionary*, is 'the accomplishment of an aim or purpose'. Both of those – the aim and the purpose, and even the idea of accomplishment – are associated with an end game, a goal, a sense of finality – a destination. The *OED* gives a further definition: 'the attainment of fame, wealth, or social status'. The attainment of an objective therefore is akin to the reaching of a particular milestone, be that notoriety, riches or the upper class. There isn't a hint of the journey to which many spiritualists refer.

Now, of course, one might argue that dictionaries change and evolve, just as society and the vernacular change and evolve. It is indeed conceivable that someday the *OED* will alter its definition of success to instead be about progress, improvement and development, although one can of course progress, improve and develop and still not achieve success. (Then again, since 'literally' now means anything other than, well, literally, anything can happen in the future.) For the time being, however, success is more frequently considered in the context of the 'realization of worthy goals', as the 'ability to fulfil your desires', and as 'the creation of wealth'.

Hold on a minute. From where were those last comments sourced? From none other than Chopra's book of spiritual success. Because even he can't help but concede that success is in fact connected to a destination, even if it makes us feel warm and fuzzy in the meantime to pretend it's something else.

But I'm being unfair. Chopra might be the most prominent modern proponent of this quotation, but it seems as though it originated with Arthur Ashe, one of the greatest tennis players of the twentieth century. Of course, he said this after he became the number one tennis player in the world (a destination); after he was inducted into the International Tennis Hall of Fame (another destination); and after he established the Association of Men's Tennis Professionals (again, a destination).

The destination-like nature of success is further emphasised by the way it is measured in life, in business and at work.

In life, success is measured economically, subjectively

and socially,[26] and each of these has a destination as its focal point.

- From an economic perspective, the money in your bank account, the reality of being employed, owning your own house – all of these are destinations that, yes, may lead to further destinations (a bigger balance, a better job, an investment property), but their capacity to compound doesn't detract from the fact they're initially a targeted ideal.

- From a subjective perspective, each individual has a mixture of positive and negative feelings about life. If those feelings are predominantly negative at the present moment and you desire a life in which those feelings are mostly positive, then that desired end state where the positives outweigh the negatives is your destination. The journey comprises the steps you'll take to get there. And regardless of whether those steps take a day, a year or a decade, and whether they necessitate hard work or no work at all, they're still steps that lead along a path, at the end of which you arrive at, yes, your destination.

---

26   E. Diener & E. Suh, 1997, 'Measuring quality of life: economic, social, and subjective indicators', *Social Indicators Research*, vol. 40, no. 1, pp. 189–216.

- From a social perspective, objective indicators such as your life span, your education, the human rights you have – all of these, too, are inherently destinations. You either live to be 100 or you don't. You either complete your degree or you don't. You either attain the freedom you desire or you don't. Success arrives dressed as an achievement, not as an attempt.

But perhaps nowhere is success defined more rigorously than in business, where managers are held responsible for any number of metrics, or – dare I say it – key performance indicators. There are apparently 75 of these KPIs that 'every manager needs to know',[27] ranging from profit to customer retention, from market share to brand equity, from cost per lead to employee engagement, from waste reduction to product recycling. The profit you want, the number of customers you need to retain, the market share you aspire to have, the brand you wish to build, the costs you'd like to minimise, the level of employee engagement you're trying to reach – each metric is a target, an end game, a point at which you can sit back and say, 'Yes, I've done it.'

---

27   B. Marr, 2012, *Key Performance Indicators (KPI): The 75 measures every manager needs to know*, Pearson Education, Harlow.

The workplace is clearly not exempt from consideration. Are you yearning for a promotion? Are you eager to learn a new skill? Are you waiting for long-service leave? Are you trying to influence your boss to accept your idea? Are you managing an important project? Each question has as its answer a destination. Maybe middle management for the first. Perhaps conflict resolution for the second. Could be a year away for the third. Might be a new product for the fourth. Perhaps a new IT system for the fifth. All will, you hope, culminate in the pleasant realisation that you have attained what you have been yearning and planning for. You will have (literally) arrived at your destination.

So a more accurate representation of this quotation is this:

'Success is a destination, and sometimes multiple destinations on the way to a larger one.'

A similar argument can be made for the following quotation:

'Love is a journey, not a destination.'

The phrase 'love is a journey' is what is known as a conceptual metaphor, meaning it creates the context in which more specific metaphors can be used. It does this by providing other metaphors with 'constraining image schema that includes a starting place, a path, and an ending place'.[28] In other words, a beginning, a middle and a destination. For example, when people refer to their new relationship as 'being on the right track', they're using a specific metaphor to describe the beginning of their romance. When they refer to their relationship as 'hitting a roadblock' or as 'smooth sailing', they're describing it in the context of the path they're currently travelling on. And when they say things like 'look how far we've come', they've generally reached a destination of some sort and are now reflecting on the journey they've experienced in getting to that point. So, in effect, love is undeniably a journey, but the simple fact of it being a journey also classifies it, in part, as a destination.

Even the concept of 'falling in love' denotes the catapulting from one metaphorical position to the next. To go from one particular situation – not being in love – to another situation – being in love – is effectively to find yourself at a new destination. It is therefore 'the process

---

28   P. Eubanks, 2000, *A War of Words in the Discourse of Trade: The rhetorical constitution of metaphor*, Southern Illinois University Press, Carbondale and Edwardsville.

of pair bonding in humans' that necessitates a process beginning with 'the subjective experience of falling in love, which sometimes leads to the establishment of long-lasting relationships'. Both of those are inherently destinations. Once you realise you've fallen in love – a feeling that oftentimes catches you by surprise – you've reached a destination. Once you formally label your pairing as a relationship, you've reached another destination. Sure, the love during this period may intensify, but it is love that usually reaches a crescendo – be it the first kiss, the first sexual experience, the proposal, the marriage, the golden anniversary (each of which is yet another destination). This is why studies, such as those from which the quotations in this paragraph have been derived,[29] have found that people also show a hormonal reaction to falling in love.

Of the people who were studied, those classified as being in love had reported higher levels of cortisol, which can reflect the 'arousal associated with the initiation of a social contact'. When the participants were tested again 18 months later, the researchers discovered the levels of cortisol had diminished, to such a degree that there was now no difference between those who

---

29   D. Marazziti & D. Canale, 2004, 'Hormonal changes when falling in love', *Psychoneuroendocrinology*, vol. 29, no. 7, pp. 931–936.

were in a relationship and those who were not. This indicates that the hormonal changes were 'probably related to some physical and/or psychological features typically associated with falling in love'. To put it another way, the destination of falling in love is a manifestation of both psychological and physical features.

Proponents of 'love as a journey, not a destination' also argue that the concept is less about falling in love and more about simply loving. They often suggest that to love is a conscious decision one makes. Anyone can choose to become more loving – to other people, to animals, to nature, to life. But barring how unrealistic that concept is especially when taking into account the traumatic events in one's life that may make one less able to love freely, even the act of choosing to love is inherently the reaching of a destination.

This is best explained by the belief that 'in order to be loving, one must love oneself. In order to love oneself, one needs to responsibly meet one's needs.'[30] This need fulfilment can comprise a number of different factors. In a relationship, it might first require the need of friendship or laughter or comfort with another person,

---

30   E. Mickel & C. Hall, 2012, 'Choosing to love: basic needs and significant relationships', *International Journal of Reality Therapy*, vol. 28, no. 2, pp. 24–27.

the existence of which enables the relationship to prosper. Or, perhaps most acutely, the need demanding fulfilment could be one's own self-esteem, confidence or health.

The point is this: while it's true that to love is often a continuous journey, due to the need to keep that love strong and constant over time (or due to the effort required to attain love in the first place), it is also just as true that to reach a point where one is either in love, or just simply loving, necessitates the reaching of destinations. These might be the fulfilment of a particular need, the instigation of a hormonal reaction or the climax that comes from reaching a new milestone.

Which, therefore, leads to the following logical adaptation:

'Love is both a journey and a destination.'

One last example before we put this adaptable quotation to bed:

'Education is a journey, not a destination.'

For the majority of people, education is an endeavour pursued for reasons other than enjoyment. They pursue it because they hope it will generate a work-related outcome they desire. The right qualification will enable them to get to a specific hierarchical or experiential destination in the workforce. It is therefore 'a professional imperative' that colleges and universities pursue the 'moral purpose of education: to make each of our graduates a productive citizen in the 21st century economy. This is preparing our students for success, not only in learning but also in their life endeavors after school'[31] – which infers that this might be the students' first full-time job, their first promotion, their new career, each of which is clearly a destination of some sort.

Even the word 'graduate', if we revert back to the trusted *OED*, is a verb that means to 'successfully complete an academic degree, course of training, or high school'. To successfully complete something, then, represents the reaching of a destination. Yes, there might have been a long journey to get to that point, and the pedant might say that the journey involved continuous learning, but one has only ever obtained an education once that journey is well and truly complete. A medical student may have learned a lot about medicine, but she

---

31   C. Kivunja, 2014, 'Do you want your students to be job-ready with
     21st Century skills? Change pedagogies: a pedagogical shift from
     Vygotskyian social constructivism to critical thinking, problem
     solving and Siemens' digital connectivism', *International Journal
     of Higher Education*, vol. 3, no. 3, pp. 81–91.

hasn't obtained a medical education until she has completed her degree. A law student may have learned a lot about the legal profession but he hasn't obtained a legal education until he has completed his degree. Learning may have taken place throughout the whole process, but unless the award is conferred, the destination of education is still far off in the distance.

And even when 'learning' and 'education' are used interchangeably, in the everyday vernacular they represent the same thing: the acquisition of knowledge and skills. To acquire something is to move from one state (of not having a valued item) to another state (of actually having it). It's about movement from one destination to another.

When we learn something new, we're experiencing 'the difference between then and now' – what we knew then and what we now know. But when, as a result of learning, we *become* someone better or something greater, that act of becoming represents 'the movement from then to now' – the reaching of a desired destination. 'Becoming is brought about by the . . . movement away from a previous moment [and] the creation of a new and different moment'.[32] Boundaries are broken.

---

32   S.R. Clegg, M. Kornberger & C. Rhodes, 2005, 'Learning / Becoming / Organizing', *Organization*, vol. 12, no. 2, pp. 147–167.

New systems are built. Fresh competencies emerge. In effect, a destination has been reached, irrespective of the fact that sometimes that destination can be unstable, disruptive or unmanageable.

So let's find a more apt reconfiguration of this quotation as well:

'Learning is a journey, and education its destination.'

7

DISPROVING THE UNHEALTHINESS OF HEALTH

n a world where obesity has become a bigger problem, literally, than poverty, it's concerning that people still give credit to the negligent rhetoric of the American jurist Oliver Wendell Holmes – **'If you wish to keep as well as possible, the less you think about your health the better'** – or Benjamin Franklin – **'Nothing is more fatal to health than an over care of it'**. In a more jovial spin on things, there are those who don't necessarily condemn the prioritisation of health, but make a mockery of it for its supposed party-pooperism. These include the Irish novelist Laurence Sterne – **'People who are always taking care of their health are like misers who are hoarding a treasure** which they have never spirit enough to enjoy' – British broadcaster Clement Freud – 'If you resolve to give up smoking, drinking and loving, you don't actually live longer; it just seems longer' – and the American humourist Josh Billings, in a not-so-humorous and ungrammatical riposte: 'There's lots of people in this world who spend so much time watching their health that they haven't the time to enjoy it.' If only they were right. For if they were, we could just abandon physical exercise, drink beer all day, gorge on a diet of sugar, and remark, through what was left of our teeth, on how enjoyable life is, even though we can no longer get off our chairs.

That those quotations are even considered motivational is odd. Each one can be found via a Google Images search, sometimes with a background of a mountaintop, at other times an array of clouds, a seaside or someone doing yoga. Surely motivators should be motivating people to get fit and healthy, rather than the reverse? It takes more effort, one would think, to live well than to live unwell.

And yet here we are, in an era in which we know categorically, via evidence-based scientific analyses, that eating well and exercising regularly decreases heart disease, diminishes diabetes-related complications, reduces the risk of cancer, combats fatigue, improves quality of life, enhances mood, extends life expectancy, alleviates the effects of arthritis, strengthens muscular movement, cuts down rates of erectile dysfunction, settles lower back pain, ramps up workplace productivity, lessens the need for prescription medication, settles anxiety, eases depressive symptoms, enriches emotional wellbeing, conquers stress, elevates cognitive performance, stems age-related problems, boosts self-esteem and pushes life satisfaction up. And yet a majority of the 'world population continues to engage in sedentary lifestyles' that neglect the simple fact that 'exercise and physical activity are associated with both physical and mental-health benefits across several diseases and diverse subpopulations'.[33] Perhaps because they're taking advice from those who think there's more to be gained from a life of neglect, where the unhappy side-effects are merely temporary distractions in an otherwise joyous life.

But, look, it's possible that life satisfaction has less to do with looking after your physical self and more to do with other factors, such as whether or not you're single, whether or not you're an immigrant, whether

---

33   F.J. Penedo & J.R. Dahn, 2005, 'Exercise and well-being: a review of mental and physical health benefits associated with physical activity', *Current Opinion in Psychiatry*, vol. 18, no. 2, pp. 189–193.

or not you're employed, and whether or not you're well educated.

Or not.

One study of thousands of people compared all of those factors and found that 'perceiving oneself to be in good health is the major predictor of being satisfied with life as a whole'. Indeed, it isn't just a major predictor of life satisfaction, but a 'massive positive predictor'. (Honestly, as soon as you have academics using words like 'massive' to describe an empirical relationship, when usually they're quite conservative with their superlatives, you know it's worth paying attention.) Unsurprisingly, then, it makes perfect sense that there is a 'relatively greater likelihood that people in poor health will have a low level of satisfaction' with their life.[34]

So when people start saying things like 'come on, live a little' and 'you only live once' as reasons why others should follow their lead and opt for a hamburger over a salad, a glass of wine over a glass of water, or the pub over the gym, it's worth thinking that it's actually *because* we only live once that we should look after

---

34 R. Melin, K.S. Fugl-Meyer & A.R. Fugl-Meyer, 2003, 'Life satisfaction in 18- to 64-year-old Swedes: in relation to education, employment situation, health and physical activity', *Journal of Rehabilitation Medicine*, vol. 35, no. 2, pp. 84–90.

ourselves, and that by doing so we don't just get to live a little but a lot.

Now, you might argue that those quoted in this chapter's opening paragraph weren't necessarily saying we should refrain entirely from physical exercise and other forms of wellness activities, but that we should be careful it doesn't turn into an obsession. While it's true that excessive exercise poses some risks – musculo-skeletal injuries, dehydration, even cardiac arrest – the reams of data that have been accumulated over the decades nonetheless indicate it is 'reasonable to con-clude that the risk exposure through physical activity is outweighed by its overall benefits'.[35] In other words, it's better to exercise a lot than not at all.

Okay, so we've established that a focus on one's physical condition leads to an almost limitless list of 'massive' benefits, and a feeling that one is generally happier with life. But what about the physical exercise itself? Is there actually enjoyment to be derived from working out and eating well? Let's find out.

One acclaimed analysis reviewed two dozen of the most respected studies on the reasons why people

---

35   K. Melzer, B. Kayser & C. Pichard, 2004, 'Physical activity: the health benefits outweigh the risks', *Current Opinion in Clinical Nutrition and Metabolic Care*, vol. 7, no. 6, pp. 641–647.

engage in physical exercise. What the researchers discovered was that even though 'most people recognised that there were health benefits associated with physical activity, this was not the main reason for participation'. Much higher on the list? Enjoyment. 'The enjoyment and social networks offered by sport and physical activity are clearly important motivators for many different groups of people aged between 18 and 50 years.' Even among older adults, who are often instructed to embark on physical exercise programs by their doctors, what keeps them going is the enjoyment that they are surprised to find they derive from it, particularly the way in which it expands their social network.[36]

Matters are a little more complicated when it comes to healthy eating. Of course, it's ridiculously enjoyable to devour a chocolate gelato or a bag of hot chips with extra salt. There's no denying the joy that comes with every bite – as does the wish that healthy food could taste that good. That's why we often resort to bad food when we're feeling crap: it temporarily makes us feel better. But does that mean healthy food tastes horrible?

---

36 S. Allender, G. Cowburn & C. Foster, 2006, 'Understanding
    participation in sport and physical activity among children and
    adults: a review of qualitative studies', *Health Education Research:
    Theory & Practice*, vol. 21, no. 6, pp. 826–835.

No, much of it is delicious. Sure, it may not be as satisfying or comforting in our hour of emotional need, but it can still be extremely delicious and indulgent. The bigger issue is that many of us are so conditioned to eating badly, either by habit or tradition or social network or income status or misleading motivational quote, that we end up taking the easy way out.

Because there's no denying the truth that eating well is not easy. It can be expensive, effortful and difficult to access. Indeed, 'that we must exercise careful, deliberate choice vis-à-vis food in order to eat healthfully is a sign that something has gone terribly wrong'.[37] The authors of that statement are scholars who emphasise that it is a moral failure in society that opportunities to consume healthy food are not as effortless as the alternatives. But its inaccessibility shouldn't detract from the fact that every healthy meal has the potential to be a mouth-watering experience rather than a cavity-inducing one.

All of which leads us to the rational conclusion that Oliver Wendell Holmes needs to have his quotation edited:

---

37   A. Barnhill, K.F. King, N. Kass & R. Faden, 2014, 'The value of unhealthy eating and the ethics of healthy eating policies', *Kennedy Institute of Ethics Journal*, vol. 24, no. 3, pp. 187–217.

'If you wish to keep as well as possible, the
more you think about your health the better.'

And Benjamin Franklin's similarly needs to be reworked:

'Nothing is more fatal to health
than to neglect it.'

Now for Laurence Sterne:

'People who are always taking care of
their health are holding a treasure which
is theirs to enjoy.'

Clement Freud:

'If you resolve to give up smoking and
drinking, you will actually live longer.'

Josh Billings:

'There are lots of people in this world who
spend so much time watching their health
that they end up with more time to enjoy it.'

8

'THE PURPOSE OF LIFE IS A LIFE OF PURPOSE'

–ROBERT BYRNE

'd never previously heard of Robert Byrne, despite having come across his famous quotation in countless variations over the years. Not that it matters. Millions of people on this globe are far more familiar with his work as a billiards expert than they are with me and my work as . . . okay, let's move on. It's quite possible that Byrne achieved remarkable things in his life because he pursued them in accordance with what he thought was his divine purpose. But I've always thought an argument based on exceptions, on outliers, isn't really an argument at all. It's a desperate attempt to cling to some credibility by clutching onto an instance, no matter how remote, that justifies one's point of view.

Which is why those who use their own lives as exemplary examples – 'If I can do it, you can too!' – are truly nauseating, because while it may be perfectly true that they have achieved what they've achieved thanks to one specific factor, such as purpose, the sad reality is that's not a realistic option for the rest of us. It may be inspiring. It may be motivational. It may be purposeful. But it isn't necessarily realistic. And it certainly isn't practical. For those who are fortunate to discover their life purpose, and subsequently to live in accordance with it – great! I'm happy for you. The rest of us, however, need to get used to the fact that perhaps there is no purpose *in* life and there is no purpose *to* life. We're here to live and breathe. We're here to do our best. We're here just because. And there isn't anything wrong with that.

Having said that, I'd rather live with purpose than without it. We all probably would. There are many studies demonstrating that purpose-driven individuals live longer, are happier and healthier, have greater self-confidence and recover more easily from a range of afflictions such as alcoholism, physical injury and even sleep disturbance. History's best example of the power of purpose is Dr Viktor Frankl. He was a psychiatrist imprisoned in the Auschwitz concentration camp, and during his time there he closely observed his own and his fellow inmates' reactions to their incarceration.

He concluded that even in brutal conditions character-ised by pain and loss and humiliation, human beings can still endure suffering if they're able to derive mean-ing from their experience, and if they have a purpose greater than themselves for which to live. His haunting and life-affirming book, *Man's Search for Meaning*, is among the most revered of the twentieth century.

So this chapter isn't a criticism of having life pur-pose. There's infinitely more research espousing the value of purpose than there is in the converse. Instead, this chapter is concerned with Robert Byrne's asser-tion that living a purposeful life is purposely the way we should be living it – if that makes sense . . . and to me it does not. Yes, one may be happier and healthier in the presence of purpose, but that doesn't mean that one needs purpose in order to be happy and healthy, or that happiness and health are dependent on purpose.

Take, for example, a study of the role that purpose played in the lives of women as they aged, particularly beyond 60. While it's true many of the participants expe-rienced a gentler transition into an older age bracket thanks to the meaningful goals that came with simple purposes such as gardening and volunteering, or more taxing purposes such as caregiving, at the same time there were women who achieved a genuine sense of ful-filment without having a purpose at all. They 'oriented their lives more toward wonder and appreciation than toward purpose. They are particularly noteworthy for their departure from the prevailing values of our contemporary mainstream culture.'[38]

What is that contemporary mainstream culture? Well, it's one that dictates that the primary way to achieve fulfilment, enlightenment or any other modern buzzword is via the setting and achievement of momentous goals. Which may be fine for some people. For others, 'deep appreciation of today, as it is, becomes the center around which they experience fulfillment and satisfaction. More focused on "being" than "becoming," they are immersed in where they are – their home, their town, their companion, working on their art – more than on planning how to make the most of these. This orientation has much to offer.' Indeed it does. As the researchers conclude, purpose 'is not for the majority'.

It's a concept alternatively referred to as 'meaning'. While for a fortunate few their meaning/purpose in life is clearly articulated, for many others that's not the case. And the consequences associated with pursuing these idealistic and perhaps unrealistic objectives can

---

38   V. Mitchell & R.M. Helson, 2016, 'The place of purpose in life in women's positive aging', *Women & Therapy*, vol. 39, no. 1–2, pp. 213–234.

induce anxiety. In one study, more than 200 university students were profiled. While many researchers survey their students simply because it's convenient to do so, in this case the selection of respondents was especially useful because university students are ordinarily at high risk of what's academically known as 'career indecision'. This term simply refers to those who are unable to figure out what to do with their life and, as a consequence, are afflicted by anxiety. Where once young adults joined the workforce and were content with whatever job they could find, it's a very different story these days. Now, society and popular media inflict upon people the necessity to find not just a job but a meaningful job; not just a career but a career in line with one's passions; not just an employer but an employer in line with one's values. All these are noble goals but, as you can imagine, they are also incredibly anxiety-inducing decisions because how many of us, especially in our twenties (or even our fifties and sixties and seventies), are abundantly clear on our true meaning and passions and values? I'd hazard a guess and say not many.

Anyway, 200 university students were surveyed to see whether the anxiety associated with career indecision is diminished when an individual has meaning or purpose in life. The answer was conditional on two important factors. First, could the individuals already say they had meaning in their life? And second, if they couldn't say they had meaning in their life, were they actively trying to find it? In regards to the first question, as expected, those who were fortunate to have already discovered a life purpose reported lower levels of anxiety. Those who were still on the lookout for this elusive meaning, though, were profoundly more anxious as a result. 'It is logical that the search for meaning in life is an anxiety provoking process,' conclude the scholars. 'Searching for meaning can cause an individual to question his or her own life structure. This process of reassessment can cause one to experience anxiety concerning unsatisfactory aspects of his or her life, including his or her career-related goals.'[39]

Now, let's say that it's only a temporary thing – something one experiences only in their twenties. Perhaps, then, we could write off career indecision as akin to growing pains – something people have to endure as part of becoming an adult. But as we know, it's very rare in this world for people to genuinely say they work in a profession associated with their life purpose. That's not to say it doesn't happen; it does, occasionally.

---

39   A.D. Miller & P.J. Rottinghaus, 2014, 'Career indecision, meaning in life, and anxiety: An existential framework', *Journal of Career Assessment*, vol. 22, no. 2, pp. 233–247.

But the vast majority of us are destined to work in jobs and industries that we frankly don't really care that much about. If we don't accept that fact of life, and if we continue to hold the fanciful notion that somewhere out there our dream job must exist, we're destined to be anxious and insecure and unhappy for a long time to come. The accidental matching of purpose with profession – the purview of the minority – is frequently used by motivational warriors to jolt us into a similar obsession, without realising that it's this very obsession that generates the anxiety in the first place. We might be better off referring to the earlier study I mentioned, which demonstrated the reality that fulfilment can actually just come from the wonder and appreciation of the everyday rather than the frenzied chase for purpose.

The same principle applies to the construct of a 'calling', which is possibly even more misleading than purpose and meaning. The notion of following your true calling has a spiritual element to it. It's effectively a declaration that you were put on this earth specifically to fulfil an important mission. It's easy to see how this plays out. Those with an unshakeable faith in a higher power might see it as their calling to dedicate their life to the poor or to the ministry. Those with a magnificent talent – surgery, for example – might see it as their calling to operate pro bono. Which is all well and good . . . except that 'research suggests calling is neither necessarily nor predictably beneficial'. That's the opening frame for a compelling scholarly analysis that identifies five paradoxes and problems on this matter:[40]

- *Necessity:* This is the perception that having a calling and pursuing it is not just desirable but essential. When the calling is eventually identified, it is rarely a matter of choice but of obligation. More often than not, this calling is in relation to paid employment of some sort, but paradoxically 'the more people accept that everyone has or should have a paid-work calling, the more [a] calling's promised meaningfulness is undermined . . . [and] when [a] calling is framed as necessary it may increase existential and psychological burdens for those who have not found, cannot enact or feel limited by their callings. Empirical work on unanswered callings demonstrates that those who have or want a calling yet cannot pursue a calling via paid work, experience frustration, depression and other negative effects.' As a result, the costs of failure

---

40 B.L. Berkelaar & P.M. Buzzanell, 2015, 'Bait and switch or double-edged sword? The (sometimes) failed promises of calling', *Human Relations*, vol. 68, no. 1, pp. 157–178.

are heightened, family members might be neglected, personal interests could be abandoned and valuable opportunities missed as people stubbornly hold on to what they think their calling ought to be.

- *Agency and control:* It is not unusual for those who have been 'called' to ignore wise advice, refuse to consider alternative options, hesitate to confront inappropriate workplace practices, open themselves up to severe overwork, and refrain from changing their mind even when faced with compelling evidence that they've made the wrong career decision. This is frequently fuelled by the pervasive contemporary discourse that makes young adults believe 'they can pursue any career they desire regardless of raw talent or potential competencies'. We often see this on talent shows where rejected aspirants are devastated because, up until that point, they had passionately believed – or been led to believe – that their true calling was to sing or dance or entertain in some way, despite a clear lack of ability. They sometimes become 'imprisoned by their own quests for self-fulfillment', or by their inflexibility to contemplate that their calling isn't really a calling, thereby rendering them to a life where they 'may not develop competencies needed to utilize a broader set of opportunities or seek new or alternative employment'. In effect, when they finally realise their calling has been misguided, they are left with few resources and skills with which to direct their energies in a different direction.

- *Inequalities:* The fact that some callings are more possible than others can entrench inequality. Some callings, for example, can only be embraced by the rich due to the funds they have at their disposal. It costs money to be taught the violin or to travel the world or to study for a medical qualification. In other cases, accepting the status quo can come to be seen as a calling, to such an extent that even those with the means to find meaningfulness hold themselves back. One prime situation where this happens is the household. Since women are lumped with a majority of the childrearing and domestic duties, an acceptance that this kind of life is their true calling ends up perpetuating the status quo – and that means fewer women in the workforce, fewer women in leadership positions, and fewer women in business and politics. Inequality, then, doesn't disappear.

- *Temporal continuity:* The construction of a calling involves the telling of a story. Stories, by and large, have a beginning, a middle and an end. They're linear. They're also internalised. They form part of an individual's identity. Which is why, when a calling doesn't go to plan – as is often the reality – it's not just that an individual's calling has been shattered. It's also that their identity suddenly becomes questionable and vulnerable. The sense of loss consequently compounds.

- *Neoliberal economics:* This is the great irony about callings. While they have underpinnings of spirituality, transcendence and social change, more often than not they are associated with capitalistic endeavours. They necessitate working long hours in organisations that capitalise on employees who think they've found their calling. They necessitate the gruelling perseverance of delusional goals that never come to fruition. And they culminate in what empirical research demonstrates is an anti-climactic fizzer: that 'those who dedicate time and resources toward their calling often fail to reap material benefits and often realize great physical and personal cost'. Their employers, however, benefit from enhanced productivity and greater profits.

Regardless, then, of whether we're talking about 'purpose', 'meaning' or 'calling', it's important for us to reframe Robert Byrne's quotation so that it better reflects the real world that most of us face. That real world is one that may generate benefits for the minority who are fortunate enough to discover their purpose, but that's something about which the rest of us definitely shouldn't be anxious and depressed. In fact, for everyone, really, this is undoubtedly a more apt reconfiguration:

'The purpose of life is simply to appreciate it.'

9

POSITIVE THINKING –
AND ALL THAT CRAP

The gifted illustrator Mary Engelbreit once said: **'If you don't like something, change it; if you can't change it, change the way you think about it.'** By reframing what you dislike as a positive, assuming such spin-doctoring were indeed possible, you'd be able to deceive yourself that things really weren't that bad. Engelbreit's supposition, however, is mild in comparison to that of Norman Vincent Peale, the famous minister and author, who exhorted his disciples thusly: **'Change your thoughts and you change your world.'** His work is not dissimilar to that of the infamously misleading book and documentary *The Secret*, which led millions to believe that if you just think positively – if you really, truly have faith in a specific ambition with all your heart – you can gain whatever it is you wish. You can manifest a mansion! You can manifest the perfect car spot! You can even manifest a career as a stand-up comedian! All you have to do is, say, put up a photo of that to which you aspire and, lo and behold, you'll have it before you can utter 'effort, luck and talent', all of which inarguably have a far greater influence on one's chances of achieving pretty much anything.

And perhaps there is nothing inherently wrong in the words of the esteemed British prime minister Winston Churchill: **'I am an optimist. It does not seem too much use being anything else.'** Except that there actually is much use in being something else, as this chapter will demonstrate. As for the American philosopher Elbert Hubbard's suggestion that **'positive anything is better than negative thinking'** – well, that isn't entirely accurate. Or positive.

Even though positive thinking was around for centuries prior to the advent of the positive psychology movement, it's quite possible it's the latter that has elevated its status and given it an aura of credibility in the eyes of those seeking an escape from reality. Martin Seligman, from whose pregnant mind the positive psychology construct was born, ascribed six so-called virtues to his ground-breaking philosophy. These were (i) wisdom and knowledge; (ii) courage; (iii) love and humanity; (iv) justice; (v) temperance; and (vi) spirituality and transcendence. One can't really argue with any of that, even though there is evidence to suggest that those virtues were generated by methods that are the antithesis of scientific rigour.[41] Regardless, it's fair to assume that wisdom ought to be valued; that courage is what's needed more of in this world; ditto with love, justice and maybe even spirituality. But to take Seligman's prized work and use it as a reason to discount the 'virtues' of its polar opposite is potentially damaging, especially when you consider that Seligman himself has written that 'positive psychology is a supplement to negative psychology, not a substitute', and that it's a practice that ordinarily comes at the cost of 'less realism'.[42] To focus exclusively on the latter discounts the benefits that arise from embracing a balance of the two. It also risks labelling the stereotyped alternative – negativity – as always detrimental to one's wellbeing, which is evidently not true at all.

---

41   B.S. Held, 2005, 'The "virtues" of positive psychology', *Journal of Theoretical and Philosophical Psychology*, vol. 25, no. 1, pp. 1–34.

42   M.E.P. Seligman, 2002, *Authentic Happiness: Using the new positive psychology to realize your potential for lasting fulfillment*, Free Press, New York.

The culmination of this is an expectation among people – and, in fact, a pervasive society-wide pressure – that we must constantly be positive, happy and optimistic, neglecting of course the impossibility of achieving that objective, and the deep sense of personal failure that comes with the realisation that one is not as positive, happy and optimistic as one ought to be.

That's not to say that working towards a state of positivity, happiness and optimism is not a worthwhile pursuit. It certainly could be, and much research proves the advantages that result, especially in relation to, say, strengthened coping mechanisms and better health. But looking at those studies on their own ignores 'a picture that is more complicated – and more useful – than "optimism is good" and "pessimism is bad"'. Especially because there are various empirically validated types of optimism and pessimism. Research has shown, for instance, that defensive pessimists (those who set 'unrealistically low expectations and then devote considerable energy to . . . reflecting on all the possible [negative] outcomes') perform just as well as strategic optimists (those who 'set optimistic expectations for their own performance and actively avoid extensive reflection'). That's because the defensive pessimists consider – and plan for – all the potentially adverse consequences. One approach isn't necessarily always better than the other.

It's just that each of us is motivated differently, such that if you were to try to cheer up a defensive pessimist, your actions would likely decrease their performance, in the same way that killing the mood of a strategic optimist is likely to affect theirs. This research 'makes clear that "one size fits all" prescriptions for optimism and negative thinking do not, in fact, fit some people very well'.[43] Or at all.

The scholars who authored that last reference go further, asserting that 'optimism and positive thinking can derail us if they lead us to ignore or discount important cues and warnings'. Their prior studies demonstrated that these cues are most acute in relation to performance. Strategic optimists, they found, were more likely to remember positive feedback, which reinforced in their mind the diminished requirement to focus on self-improvement. As usually happens when things go well, optimism gets the credit for any success – but when things fall apart, as they often do, personal blame is frequently avoided.

Now let's move away from optimism and pessimism for a moment and focus on what is a more common occurrence: bad moods. These are the intense

---

43   J.K. Norem & E.C. Chang, 2002, 'The positive psychology of negative thinking', *Journal of Clinical Psychology*, vol. 58, no. 9, pp. 993–1001.

short-lived episodes that seemingly have no cause, but which the rah-rah positive types would have you believe should be avoided if you want to maximise your powers of manifestation. A number of academic studies, however, indicate quite strongly that being in a bad mood can actually generate a number of specific outcomes that can be deemed beneficial in a variety of contexts.[44]

- The first (and strongest) is an improved memory. That's because those who feel grumpy tend to pay closer attention to their surroundings. In one experiment, shoppers were asked to recall the features of a store they had just visited. Those who were surveyed on cold, rainy days were able to recollect the store's interior in remarkable detail. Those who were surveyed on sunny, warm days weren't able to remember as much. This heightened attention also means that those who are feeling temporarily negative are less likely to take on board false or misleading information, which tends to infiltrate happier people at a far greater rate.

---

44 J.P. Forgas, 2013, 'Don't worry, be sad! On the cognitive, motivational, and interpersonal benefits of negative mood', *Current Directions in Psychological Science*, vol. 22, no. 3, pp. 225–232.

- The second characteristic is improved judgemental accuracy. An example of that is when we form judgements based on an initial perception we develop, thereby ignoring information that comes afterwards, which may actually be in conflict with the judgement we've prematurely set in concrete. In one experiment, judges were asked to form an impression about an individual based on details that described the person as either an extrovert or an introvert. A bias was certainly present – unless the judge was in a negative mood, in which case the bias was 'completely eliminated', thereby resulting in fairer judgements.

- The third is reduced gullibility. Perhaps nowhere is this more obvious than when people are confronted by urban myths, rumours and deception. In one experiment, those who were feeling sad were less likely to accept facial expressions as genuine, which meant they were at less risk of being deceived. In another experiment, when sad participants watched a recording of an interrogation, they were better at accurately identifying those who were being insincere.

- The fourth is reduced stereotyping. In what is inherently a confronting experiment, the researchers asked happy and sad people to shoot at other people (in a simulation, of course) who they thought were carrying guns. Some of those targets were made to look Muslim. The result was that there 'was a significantly greater tendency overall to shoot at Muslims; however, negative [moods] actually *reduced*, and positive [moods] *increased*, this discriminative tendency'. The reason was the same as that noted above: negative people are more cognisant of detail.

- The fifth is greater motivation. When sad and happy people were given a challenging task to complete, those who felt sad persevered longer at the task and got more of it correct.

- The sixth may sound counterintuitive, but here it is anyway. Those in a negative state of mind are actually the beneficiaries of interpersonal advantages, such as, surprisingly, politeness. That's because they're more inclined to phrase their requests in a cautious manner, taking care to set their preferences articulately.

- Now here's the seventh: increased fairness. Experiments have shown that positive people tend to be more selfish, whereas negative people tend to be more equitable. In various games, during which participants had to share resources they had accumulated, it was the happier folk who were more inclined to hoard their kitty for themselves. Negative people, in contrast, were more likely to share it around.

- And here's another: more effective persuasion. There was one experiment in which happy and sad people were asked to write persuasive arguments, such as a letter to students making the case for an increase in school fees. You can predict the result, I'm sure. Those who were classified as sad were able to outperform their happier colleagues. 'Their arguments featured more concrete and tangible information', the scholar found; also, 'arguments produced by sad persuaders actually worked better in producing real attitude change in naïve participants'.

If we look at the aforementioned benefits in unison – memory, judgement, non-gullibility, anti-discrimination, motivation, politeness, fairness and persuasiveness – it isn't too much of a stretch to conclude that, actually, negative thinking can be quite beneficial for one's future success. For these findings, we have to thank Professor Joseph Forgas of the University of New South Wales, who would have to be Australia's (and perhaps the world's) most eminent researcher into the realities of a bad mood: the fact that it isn't really all that bad, and that 'the unrelenting pursuit of happiness may often be self-defeating'.

So the next time someone patronisingly tells you to smile more or to just think positive thoughts, don't believe them right away. They might have a point, but their absolutist messages are most probably hollow.

All this leads us, then, to reconfigure the motivational quotes that began this chapter. Mary Engelbreit's is more accurate when it's edited in the following way:

> **'If you don't like something, change it;**
> **if you can't change it, free yourself of it.'**

Norman Vincent Peale's is better off like this:

> **'Change your thoughts and you risk**
> **changing your realistic sense of the world.'**

Even though I'm reticent to edit the great Winston Churchill, I must:

> **'I am an optimist. It does not seem too**
> **much use being anything else, unless one**
> **values memory, judgement, non-gullibility,**

**anti-discrimination, motivation, politeness,
fairness and persuasiveness.'**

Elbert Hubbard, too, needs to have his quotation reworded:

**'Positive anything is not necessarily better
than negative thinking. Context is what
determines which is more appropriate.'**

Ah, that's better. All of a sudden I feel much more positive.

10

'LIFE IS TOO SHORT TO WAKE UP WITH REGRETS'

—PAULO COELHO

There is something incredible – as in, not credible – about people who claim they don't have any regrets. It's as though they haven't kicked themselves, even just once, over an unforced error, a humiliating mistake, a self-inflicted faux pas. Or if they acknowledge that they have found themselves, once or twice, in these scary and scarring situations, they have since profoundly interpreted their war wounds as fond reminders of who they've become, how much they've changed, what they've learned. Yes, I say, that may be well and good, but those experiences are still regrets. You might not want to turn back time and undo them, but they are still regrets. No, they often retort. These are learning experiences, character-building moments, defining stages of life that can't possibly be classified in that embarrassing and humbling category labelled Regret. And so here we are again, I invariably ponder, where people use semantics and wordplay, skewing reality to get around the stark confrontation that comes with publicly acknowledging they've stuffed up.

As an aside, my day job is as a senior leader in quite a large business, which means recruitment is a task I spend quite a bit of time doing as my team grows and evolves. Invariably, I'll ask a simple question in each interview, which goes a little something like this: *What would you say is your biggest work-related regret?* Very few people are brave enough to answer it honestly. The vast majority – almost all of them, in fact – sit there for a painfully long period of time, thinking of some suitable regret to offer up. I suspect these individuals fall into two general response types. There's the type that lacks self-awareness, which means they don't spend much time reflecting on their successes and failures – which is why they struggle to come up with a good example. The other type probably has several major regrets but is too afraid to admit them, lest they look bad. In these interviews I try to help them out, stating that I can honestly list a dozen significant regrets I've had just in the past six months. Sometimes I'll even declare one or two.

But very rarely are candidates willing to offer one of their own. At fault, I believe, are quotations and mindsets such as this chapter's affirmation by Paulo Coelho, which seem to shame us into making secrets of our regrets – even though what they represent, and what I'm looking for in job interviews, is nothing more than an example of self-awareness and self-improvement.

Outside of the interview room, this phenomenon might best be explained by the tendency for people to think that if they acknowledge their regrets – and, worse, make them public – they're essentially wallowing in grief and remorse. What's done is done, they think. And that's fine. It's one thing to leave the past in the past. It's another to pretend it didn't happen.

This manufactured denial can be attributed to a term known as 'possible selves'. Your possible self is the personal characterisation you have in your imagination, which depicts who you hope to be in the future, what you'll look like and what you'll have as a result of achieving a particular life goal. It's quite a motivating idea, because it comprises not just goals but also all the future experiences you expect will mould you into the self you most want to be at some determined point in time. But when an unexpected turn of events, either self-inflicted or otherwise, threatens your possible self, or maybe even demolishes it, regret often ensues.

It was that concept of lost possible selves that prompted researchers in one particular study to interview dozens of participants with this as the underlying question: 'How great would your life have been if only . . .' *If only* is the key term here. Even when the situation is beyond our control, regret can still be a consequence. But is it possible, despite the presence of regret, and the distress that commonly follows, for regret to be something that one doesn't necessarily . . . well, regret? That's what the researchers wanted to discover, and so they looked at two positive outcomes that might be derived from regret. One was happiness; the other was ego development.

The definition of happiness is self-explanatory; whereas the definition of ego development probably needs some elaboration, because chances are it's not what you initially suspect. The word 'ego' can be misleading. It isn't necessarily about being egotistical but about building character, maturity and complexity in who we are and who we will become. In this particular study, three areas of potential regret were investigated:[45]

---

45   L.A. King & J.A. Hicks, 2007, 'Whatever happened to "what might have been"? Regrets, happiness, and maturity', *American Psychologist*, vol. 62, no. 7, pp. 625–636.

- How great would your life have been if only you hadn't gotten divorced?

- How great would your life have been if only your child didn't have Down syndrome?

- How great would your life have been if only you were straight and not gay?

In each of those scenarios, dwelling on regret had an adverse impact on happiness. Not so with ego development. For example, parents who had children with Down syndrome were found, on talking about the 'possible self' they had lost, to have enriched their ego development, because they were able to reflect on how they had evolved as a result of raising a child with an intellectual disability. Similarly, gay participants who could elaborate on the heterosexual possible self they once prized were better off – from an ego perspective – as a result. So too were women who, with the passage of time, were able to describe their experiences of divorce vividly. They didn't deny their regret. They accepted it and spoke openly about it. These findings remained constant even when the participants were interviewed again two years later. The scholars concluded: 'The individual who has made him or herself vulnerable

to acknowledged regret can be seen to adopt a coura-
geous stance toward life: Despite acknowledging the
risks of expecting anything from life, the happy and
complex person maintains a heroic commitment to
continue to do just that.' In other words, regret isn't seen
as an unfavourable emotion, but as a necessary marker
of what makes us human.

Another term that explains the phenomenon is
'counterfactual thinking'. A counterfactual, in the context of regret, is when you look back at a particular
event and recognise it could have panned out more
favourably had you made a different decision, taken
an alternative action or said something you hadn't
said. Turning that into a counterfactual thought means
changing your behaviour in some way, in the hope that
the previous negative consequences might be avoided
in the future. For example, consider a student who fails
a subject because he left his assignment until the last
minute. His counterfactual thought might then be that,
from then on, he would always start working on his
assignments at least a week before they were due.

With that as background information, I'd now like
to share with you the findings of research that compared the emotion of regret with 11 other emotions
that are ordinarily considered negative. These were:
guilt, sadness, disappointment, shame, fear, disgust,

anger, frustration, anxiety, jealousy and boredom. The researchers wanted to see which of these 12 emotions was most likely to result in a range of productive outcomes, such that the emotion itself, while temporarily negative, ends up actually being somewhat positive. They investigated five such positive outcomes. Of the 12 emotions, regret came first in all five outcomes.[46] Here's an overview:

- *Counterfactual Thinking I:* One variety of counterfactual thinking is known as the 'approach' method. The example noted above, about a student behaving differently as a result of a regret, emerged in this study as being most evident among the regretful. And certainly more so than among those feeling jealousy and boredom.

- *Counterfactual Thinking II:* Another variety of counterfactual thinking is known as 'avoidance', which is when an individual refrains from indulging in a particular behaviour. In the example noted above, regret might prompt the avoidance of activities such as

---

46   C. Saffrey, A. Summerville & N.J. Roese, 2008, 'Praise for regret: People value regret above other negative emotions', *Motivation & Emotion*, vol. 32, no. 1, pp. 46–54.

late-night parties, peer pressure and procrastination in order to perform better at school. In the study, this version of counterfactual thinking similarly emerged most profoundly among the regretful, and certainly more so than among the jealous or the bored.

- *Sense-making:* This occurs when the feeling of a specific emotion helps you to make sense of – to interpret and to understand – a particular event you've experienced. In this study, again, those who were dealt a dose of regret were more likely to leverage it for the purposes of more thoroughly understanding what they had just endured – more so than those, for example, who had experienced anxiety or frustration.

- *Social harmony:* When a negative emotion is perceived to generate a social benefit, such as bringing people closer together or enhancing the effectiveness of a team, social harmony is the by-product. In this study, evidence of social harmony was more likely to be reported among the regretful. Not so much among the angry or disgusted.

- *Insight:* This one is probably self-explanatory. It involves self-reflection and analysis, with the expectation that it will lead to some sort of personal improvement. Well, of the five positive outcomes, it was in this one that regret appeared the strongest, way ahead of its other negative counterparts, such as boredom, anxiety, jealousy or anger.

'Regret appears to be an emotion that people perceive to have a wide range of positive benefits,' write the scholars. 'People value their regret experience. They value it in both an absolute sense (the favorable aspects outweigh the unfavorable aspects) and in a relative sense (as compared to other commonly experienced negative emotions).'

That is particularly good to know because, in the same study, regret was found to be the most frequent negative emotion the participants experienced. This highlights the danger of accepting quotations like the one from the ordinarily wise Paulo Coelho. When a specific emotion is so prevalent throughout our life, and indeed throughout our day, there is greater merit in embracing that emotion, understanding it and interpreting it, than there is in vilifying it or trying to abolish it.

Let's move on now to a specific type of self-inflicted regret, one of those with which all of us are undoubtedly familiar: the career regret. Employees are changing jobs at a faster rate than ever before. And it's not just jobs – it's also professions, with some estimates suggesting that many people, particularly those of the younger generations, can expect to have between seven and 14 careers throughout their lifetime. With such chopping and changing, it's inevitable that we'll stuff something up along the way. We'll say yes to the wrong job or no to the right one, and forever kick ourselves for having been so foolish.

This was demonstrated in a survey of almost 1500 people conducted by researchers investigating two distinct types of career regrets: objective and subjective.[47] Objective career regrets are those associated with extrinsic matters, such as the actions that have resulted in not having earned enough, or not having been promoted as far up the corporate hierarchy as we wanted. Subjective career regrets are those that have less to do with materialism and more to do with intrinsic benefits, such as personal development and spiritual fulfilment.

The researchers discovered that people often acknowledged they harboured objective career regrets

---

47   S.E. Sullivan, M.L. Forret & L.A. Mainiero, 2007, 'No regrets? An investigation of the relationship between being laid off and experiencing career regrets', *Journal of Managerial Psychology*, vol. 22, no. 8, pp. 787–804.

when they switched from organisation to organisation. Subjective career regrets, meanwhile, were the domain of those who had made a job change for family reasons, rather than strategic job-related purposes. Being laid off, as might be expected, came with consequences that were both objective and subjective. In any case, 'the regrets individuals have may influence their career behaviors and transition decisions [in the future], resulting in different approaches to their work and their lives'. In other words, acknowledging a career regret can pay dividends, even if it hurts temporarily. What's required first, however, is a simple nod towards the unavoidable fact that a regret exists.

Paulo Coelho's quotation, therefore, seems more legitimate when one simple three-letter word is inserted:

'Life is too short to not wake up with regrets.'

11

DREAMS CAN COME TRUE ... AND OTHER FORMS OF SELF-DECEPTION

From a purely statistical perspective, there should be no debate, no argument, no doubting whatsoever the simple fact that dreams do not come true for 99.9999 per cent of the population. And that's a conservative estimate. In the meantime, the 0.0001 per cent of people fortunate enough to become, say, a movie star or a pop icon tirelessly blabber that if their fans just believed in themselves, then their dreams, too, can come true. Which is obviously not true. Because often their fans' dreams are similarly about fame and fortune, neither of which is even remotely likely when they can't sing, can't act, can't dance and look like a normal person.

And even if they can sing, can act, can dance and look spectacular, there's very little room at the apex of super-stardom for all the desperate wannabes. This isn't just about the entertainment industry, of course. Billionaires fool budding investors; CEOs entice up-and-coming managers; business titans lure new entrepreneurs; presidents tantalise political aspirants. In every case, dreamers are made to believe first in their dreams, and then in themselves, leading to a stubborn case of self-deception.

Which isn't to say that dreams should be unpursued. They're fine so long as they're limited to giving their conjurer something to focus on rather than something to obsess over. It's the latter that frequently leads to self-deception; why would you invest every ounce of energy, and sacrifice so much of what you value, unless you had deceived yourself into believing without a hint of doubt that you were destined for the greatness you have in your dreams?

The dreams themselves aren't the issue. We all have them. They provide stimulus and excitement. What makes them perilous, and their advocates misleading, is when we assume that they must be achieved at any cost, and that we're the rightful owner of the prize they promise. Suddenly, they aren't just dreams; they're a calling. Especially when they're voiced in terms such as those by Walt Disney: **'If you dream it, you can do it.'** And what such an unflinching position necessitates is extreme belief to the point of self-deception, particularly when Norman Vincent Peale says, **'Believe in yourself! Have faith in your abilities'**; when Diana Ross says, **'In the end, you really just need to believe in yourself'**; when Venus Williams says, **'You have to believe in yourself when no one else does – that makes you a winner right there'**; when Christian Louboutin says, **'You need to believe in yourself and what you do'**; when Jon Bon Jovi says, **'Believe in yourself. Believe in your dreams. If you don't, who will?'**

You get the picture. It really is a slippery slope of self-deception – although some might say, 'So what? Even if people are deceiving themselves, is that such a bad thing?' Well, yeah, it is.

One reason is that self-deception blocks us from accepting important information about ourselves. One scholarly analysis, for instance, stated 'the most appropriate generalization we can truthfully make of self-deceivers . . . is that they are guided by a desire to believe'. That desire to believe infers that they frequently block the nagging suspicions – the implicit knowledge – that arises from the continued rejections from modelling agencies, or the repeated start-up ideas that fail, or the novel that still hasn't been picked up by publishers. And while the self-deception might once have been manufactured – 'I must believe in myself in order to become successful' – eventually it morphs into self-delusion: it's no longer just manufactured positive thinking but a genuine and unshakeable belief in one's own destiny. In any case, 'self-deceivers do not get what they want' because 'such cases are failures of self-knowledge'.[48] What that means is that, deep down, they're aware of the ugly truth. They just subconsciously choose to ignore it.

This, unsurprisingly, leads to a raft of unrealistic and personally unfair expectations. Let's look at a specific example that has been explored empirically: entrepreneurs. I was once one of them. Or an obsessively aspiring one, at least. And what I noticed among the other entrepreneurs with whom I associated was that all of us possessed the same self-help bibles written by Tony Robbins, Napoleon Hill, Michael Gerber, Robert Kiyosaki and, yes, even Donald Trump. We all had the same vision, too. Many millions of dollars. Long holidays. The freedom to choose our own hours. A job aligned to our passions. In almost every case, our new ventures didn't make anywhere near as much money as we could earn as salaried workers.

---

48 E. Funkhouser, 2005, 'Do the self-deceived get what they want?', *Pacific Philosophical Quarterly*, vol. 86, no. 3, pp. 295–312.

And the extraordinary holidays for which we once yearned didn't exist at all (even as just plain old ordinary holidays). Sure, we had the freedom to choose our own hours, but that was only because we were unhealthily working every hour just to keep our heads above water. And those passions we once adored became things we detested, because, as so frequently occurs, when you turn your passion into a business you end up commodifying something you love. Your heart sings less and less with every email, every spreadsheet, every invoice, every transaction, every complaint, every administrative activity, every call from a debt collector.

Of course, there are exceptions. There are those who strike it rich ridiculously quickly, who go on four luxury holidays a year, who work – dare I say it – a four-hour week, who truly love what they do. But they're also the ones who write the articles and the books, who speak at seminars and on television, claiming that anyone can have that same lifestyle – anyone can make their dreams come true! – if only they first believe. Well, millions upon millions of people believe. Perhaps even those extolling it do as well. It's a belief that is as uncompromising as it is vigorous. And yet nothing happens.

In one study, over 10,000 people were asked the following questions each year for a period of approximately five years:

- 'Would you say that you yourself are better off, worse off or about the same financially than you were a year ago?'

- 'Looking ahead, how do you think you yourself will be financially a year from now: better than you are now, worse off than you are now, or about the same?'

The self-employed, on average, forecast their incomes to rise by about 33 per cent higher than did salaried employees. The reality, though, was that their incomes deteriorated. Employees, in contrast, experienced an overall rise. The researchers concluded that 'the self-employed are more liable to excess optimism', and they 'do seem to be driven by wishful thinking'. The researchers go further to suggest that what underpins this unrealistic optimism, especially among men, is that they think others will be attracted to their prospect of future success. Subsequently, 'the best way to convince another of your own abilities is to really believe in them', they write.[49] Self-delusion therefore kicks in. As does a kick in the pants sooner or later.

---

49 G. Arabsheibani, D. de Meza, J. Maloney & B. Pearson, 2000, 'And a vision appeared unto them of a great profit: evidence of self-deception among the self-employed', *Economic Letters*, vol. 67, no. 1, pp. 35–41.

Does that imply we shouldn't be entrepreneurial? No. Let's start businesses. Let's take risks. Let's be innovative and daring and progressive. But let's also not believe in ourselves and our dreams to such an extent that we shut out our honest faculties, the ones that let us know, usually not so subtly, that we're on the wrong track. If only we had paid attention, the fall wouldn't have been as thunderous.

But we don't pay attention and we consequently fall. We neglect the objective data bombarding us and 'so we fool ourselves, in search of pride. [Self-deceptive] individuals think they are more talented and honest than the evidence indicates'[50] – and this, understandably, makes them happier, since ignorance is bliss. Happiness is indeed one of the benefits of self-deception. Research also indicates that to self-deceive leads to greater confidence, more risk-taking and less distraction. But at what cost? According to one series of experiments, the short-term benefits pale in comparison to the long-term costs.[51]

---

50   T. Cowen, 2005, 'Self-deception as the root of political failure', *Public Choice*, vol. 124, no. 3, pp. 437–451.

51   Z. Chance, M.I. Norton, F. Gino & D. Ariely, 2011, 'Temporal view of the costs and benefits of self-deception', *Proceedings of the National Academy of Sciences of the United States of America*, vol. 108, no. 3, pp. 15655–15659.

In the first experiment, participants were split into two groups and asked to complete a test. One group was given access to the answers. The other group was not. They were then surveyed after the test to ascertain their level of confidence ahead of the next test. Those who had been given the answers in the first test – otherwise known as the cheaters – were far more confident that they would continue to do well. In other words, they discounted the unfair advantage they had been given and instead deceived themselves 'into believing that their strong performance was a reflection of their ability'. They truly believed in themselves, despite evidence to the contrary.

In the second experiment, the researchers sought to find out whether the inflated expectations of the self-deceiving individuals materialised. As might be expected, they performed no better than the other group. They had 'deceived themselves into believing they were smarter than their results on the second test proved them to be'.

In the third experiment, the participants were told they could earn cash according to how accurately they predicted their performance on the next test. The researchers wanted to see whether monetary incentives would temper the self-deceivers a little. With money at stake, maybe their expectations would be a little less swollen. Well, not quite. Their high expectations remained the same, and their performance no better, leading the researchers to conclude that 'although self-deception can be beneficial in the short term, basing decisions on erroneous beliefs can prove costly in the longer term'.

Does all this indicate we shouldn't believe in ourselves? No. We should absolutely believe in ourselves, so long as we don't abandon our critical self-reflection in the process. Belief in oneself must be accompanied by a preparedness to admit that what we once made ourselves believe was true may no longer be the case. It's humbling to make such an admission, and it might feel defeatist, but doing so will save a lot of time, energy and money that might be better spent on other endeavours.

Therefore, let's edit the quotations that began this chapter. Walt Disney's looks better like this:

'If you dream it, you can do it. Assuming you're a character in a fairy tale.'

And Norman Vincent Peale's feels more accurate this way:

'Believe in yourself! Have faith in your abilities. Just make sure they're definitely abilities.'

Diana Ross's hits the right note when it's worded like this:

> **'In the end, you really just need to believe in yourself within reason.'**

Venus Williams hits the mark when hers is rearranged like this:

> **'You have to believe in yourself when no one else does – although if no one else does, it's probably wise to ask yourself why.'**

Christian Louboutin's fits more comfortably when adjusted like this:

> **'You need to believe in yourself and what you do, but only with a critical and honest mindset.'**

And Jon Bon Jovi's sounds about right when versed in this way:

> **'Believe in yourself. Believe in your dreams. If you don't, that's okay. You'll have others.'**

12

'IF YOU DON'T KNOW WHERE YOU ARE GOING, YOU WILL PROBABLY END UP SOMEWHERE ELSE'

–LAURENCE J. PETER

P rofessor Laurence J. Peter was the genius behind the 'Peter principle', a term that describes the rise of individuals who get promoted right up to their level of incompetence. It's at this point their career hits a ceiling, since their lack of competence suddenly becomes obvious to pretty much everyone. The focus of this chapter, however, is on Peter's other principle: that it's really important to know where you're going in life. To put it another way, it's important to have a goal to which you direct your energy, otherwise you risk finding yourself at an altogether different destination, and that, apparently, is a very, very bad thing because . . . well, goals are very, very good, which means their absence is bad, and therefore not recommended. So where you end up has to be – it just has to be – the place at which you intended to arrive, otherwise you've failed.

This is a mentality that's given rise to acronyms such as SMART – 'specific, measurable, adaptable, realistic, time-based' – so that goals are framed in such a way that they have the best chance of success. One of the more stomach-churning acronyms is BHAG, which stands for a 'big, hairy, audacious goal' – because it's not sufficient anymore to just have a simple, humble objective; these days it must be enormous. But, look, countless studies conducted over recent decades demonstrate the performance-enhancing effects of goal-setting, the culmination of which has given rise to their ubiquitous use in personal and occupational forums. Goals have indeed 'gone wild', which is what one academic analysis discovered upon reviewing their unintended consequences.[52]

One of those side-effects includes the unethical behaviour that people may be tempted to adopt in pursuit of their big, hairy and audacious goal. While the

---

52   L.D. Ordóñez, M.E. Schweitzer, A.D. Galinsky & M.H. Bazerman, 2009, 'Goals gone wild: The systematic side effects of over-prescribing goal setting', *Harvard Business Review*, Working Paper 09-083.

scholars in the aforementioned analysis focus on examples such as Enron, one only needs to look at other, more recent instances where the presence of an ambitious goal – or a 'stretch target', as it's frequently referred to in management speak – have led crusaders down the well-trodden path of avarice and sin. The Global Financial Crisis is but one example where the insatiable drive for profits and fat bonuses led salivating bankers to sacrifice decency and morals as they remorselessly engineered the bankruptcy and despondency of millions of lives.

These side-effects are made worse by the ways in which many goals prioritise short-term gains over long-term advantages; self-interest over the greater good; quantitative outcomes over harder-to-measure qualitative outcomes; winning at any cost over simply winning; and risk-taking over risk calculation. The researchers identify other factors, too, such as the 'ceiling effect', which is when employees, once they achieve a management-directed goal, take their foot off the pedal and coast for the rest of the month, or the 'negotiation effect', which is when people with a set goal during a bargaining situation are more likely to reach a point at which neither party is willing to compromise in order to progress the negotiation. It is for these reasons the scholars conclude that, 'in many situations, the damaging effects of goal setting outweigh its benefits', and that 'aggressive goal setting within an organization will foster an organizational climate ripe for unethical behavior'. Note the key word in that sentence: will. Not might or could, but will.

The scholars also make note of many other studies, which find that, yes, the setting of goals does increase performance, but the increased performance comes at a cost. Sometimes, as mentioned in the preceding paragraph, the cost is ethical behaviour and organisational culture. At other times, it's learning, self-esteem, collaboration or open-mindedness. Sometimes intrinsic motivations are lost: employees who may once have completed a task simply because they enjoy it now end up doing it for reasons associated with goal attainment; enjoyment is replaced by a shallow sense of efficient, productive and assessable execution.

Mentioned earlier, too, was the concept of the stretch goal. It could also be referred to as an impossibility goal – the kind of goal you have an almost zero chance of achieving, but to which you feel you should nonetheless aspire because you just might reach it. Or you might get close enough. This brings to mind the injunction to 'reach for the stars', which has appeared in myriad quotations, the most famous of which would have to be advertiser Leo Burnett's: 'When you reach for the stars you may not quite get one, but you won't come up with a handful of mud either.'

The potentially harmful nature of stretch goals, from an organisational perspective, was thoroughly explicated in a scholarly analysis that identified three distinct corollaries:[53]

- *Cognitive effects:* Instead of being perceived as a stimulating intellectual challenge, stretch goals frequently lead to feelings of overwhelm, impulsiveness, disorientation and disorganisation, because the organisation has neither the ability nor the resources to achieve the goal. It can also divert attention from other, more easily attainable goals.

- *Emotional effects:* The existence of a stretch goal is usually inseparable from an urgent need for significant change, which often propels employees into a negative emotional state. Emotions are notoriously contagious, the consequence of which ends up being a widespread reticence to experiment and

---

53   S.B. Sitkin, K.E. See, C.C. Miller, M.W. Lawless & A.M. Carton, 2011, 'The paradox of stretch goals: Organizations in pursuit of the seemingly impossible', *Academy of Management Review*, vol. 36, no. 3, pp. 544–566.

an endemic sense of helplessness. Motivation, too, can be diminished when employees see a particular goal as out of reach. Its impossibility, rather than giving them a tantalising hope of the future, has a demotivating effect, not only because it compels employees not to bother trying but also because the failure to reach the stretch goal can damage morale and inhibit resilience.

- *Behavioural effects:* The effort required to pursue a stretch goal can result in detrimental organisational performance in other areas, because it distracts people, consumes resources, threatens stability and impairs coordination, the combination of which can be counterproductive.

But let's put stretch goals aside for the moment and focus instead on another consequence of goals in general: their tendency to trigger destructive leadership behaviours. There are many varieties of destructive leaders. There's the bully, the tyrant, the aggressor, the underminer, the yeller, the abuser and the narcissist. And there are just as many causes of such behaviour. In some cases, the leader is a characteristically angry and hostile person, or has had a tough life and is now taking it out on others. In other cases, the work environment is the enabler of the destructive behaviour. This can include unfairness, organisational crises, interpersonal conflict, limited resources and – ah, yes – the predominance and prioritisation of goals, especially those that are linked to rewards.

One expert analysis on reward-based goals concluded that the mere existence of a reward represents a consequence – a risk 'you will probably end up somewhere else' – which heightens a leader's stress such that destructive behaviours can ensue. There are two reasons this occurs.[54] The first is that when a reward is attached to a goal, it becomes 'apparent that valued outcomes are at stake', thereby pushing up stress – due not only to the potential consequences but also to the harsh realisation that this might occur because the individual may not have the resources to meet what the situation demands. The second reason is that the reward 'can increase an individual's awareness that a potential threat of failure exists'. After all, if failure were not an option, a reward would most probably not be on offer. So stress ramps up, and so too does the likelihood of destructive behaviour.

54　　M. Bardes & R.F. Piccolo, 2010, 'Goal setting as an antecedent of destructive leader behaviour', in B. Schyns & T. Hansbrough (eds), *When Leadership Goes Wrong: Destructive leadership, mistakes, and ethical failures*, Information Age Publishing, Charlotte, pp. 3–22.

To complete this chapter, let's explore one goal in particular: the financial one. It's often an all-consuming goal characterised by an intense desire to pay off the mortgage or make your first million or retire by 40. Whatever its manifestation, it's a goal empirically found in the past to be associated with depression, anxiety and a range of behavioural disorders. It's important to note a critical distinction here. While an earlier chapter demonstrated the link between money and happiness, there's a big difference between accumulating money over time and obsessively pursuing it. Much research has found the latter to have an inverse relationship with happiness and self-esteem. For example, an analysis of almost 13,000 people tracked a number of variables from the time these individuals started college until 19 years later.[55] What the researchers discovered was that 'the stronger the financial goal, the lower the overall life satisfaction'. The existence of a financial goal might not necessarily make someone unhappy, but it certainly seems as though it makes them less happy than those with modest aspirations. There was also a

---

55   C. Nickerson, N. Schwarz, E. Diener & D. Kahneman, 2003, 'Zeroing in on the dark side of the American dream: A closer look at the negative consequences of the goal for financial success', *Psychological Science*, vol. 14, no. 16, pp. 531–536.

significant negative effect in satisfaction with family life, friendships and employment, which led the authors of the study to call such a pursuit 'the dark side of the American dream'.

Laurence J. Peter's quotation, then, probably makes more sense with the inclusion of an addendum, something a little like this:

> **'If you don't know where you are going,
> you will probably end up somewhere else –
> and that could be the best thing that ever
> happens to you.'**

13

IT'S NOT WHAT HAPPENS TO YOU ... OR IS IT?

W. Mitchell has quite a story to tell. In a motorbike accident back in the 1970s, he suffered horrific burns to most of his body, including his face. Most of his fingers were amputated. A few years later, misfortune had him in her sights once again, when a small plane he was piloting crashed, rendering him a paraplegic. Now he travels the world and delivers magnetic presentations, telling audiences that 'it's not what happens to you; it's what you do about it' that matters. There are others, too, who cite a similar refrain, despite not having a comparable life-changing experience. The American composer Terry Riley is one: 'It's not what happens to

you in life that matters; what matters is how you deal with it!' Evangelical Christian pastor Chuck Swindoll is another who I'm pretty sure didn't use robust empirical methodology to determine that **'life is 10% what happens to you and 90% how you react to it'**. Credit, though, should go to the ancient Greek philosopher Epictetus who was probably the first to claim that **'it's not what happens to you, but how you react to it that matters'**. And he should know. He was born a slave in what we now call Turkey, and was tortured by his master to such an extent he never walked properly again. He subsequently had a thriving career.

But whether or not a tragic past exists to justify the use of this motivational phrase, and irrespective of the mountains that were climbed (ugh), the barriers that were overcome (ugh again) and the adversity that was endured, the fact remains it's really not that true. The notion that life circumstances are not important, that they don't impose fundamental limits on one's life, is borderline patronising. Not even borderline patronising – just patronising.

To understand why that's the case, let's look at a scholarly work that was important for three reasons. First, it was longitudinal, which means it tracked people's wellbeing over extended periods of time – in this case up to two decades. Second, the sample size was huge: 40,000 folks in Germany and another 27,000 in the United Kingdom. Third, the analysis looked at many studies that had been completed in the recent past. What the researchers wanted to find out was whether significant life events, such as divorce and unemployment, have an impact on people's perceptions of their wellbeing. Well, what they discovered was that it takes widows and widowers approximately seven years before their satisfaction in life returns to the level it was at prior to their partner's death. For those who get divorced or lose their job, their life satisfaction never returns to the point it was at before the unexpected change. Perhaps nowhere is this more profound than for those who are suddenly hit with a permanent disability. The raft of studies leads to the conclusion that 'happiness levels do change, adaptation is not inevitable, and life events do matter'.[56]

But let's get extra-inquisitive for a moment. That study was based on people's perceptions of their own happiness, which in a way reinforces the message professed by Mitchell, Riley, Swindoll and Epictetus, which is that shit happens, and so what you have to do is stop

---

56   R.E. Lucas, 2007, 'Adaptation and the set-point model of subjective well-being: Does happiness change after major life events?', *Current Directions in Psychological Science*, vol. 16, no. 2, pp. 75–79.

feeling like a victim and instead think of yourself as a victor. In other words, snap out of it! They would easily win that argument if that meta-analysis I just mentioned was the only evidence to back up the extraordinary effect of life events beyond our control.

Let's look at another one that's much more serious: depression. Many studies in the past have found that life circumstances – such as childhood abuse, parental divorce, chronic disease and financial hardship – are all indicators of depression later in life. In an Irish study of more than 3500 people, researchers looked at some additional variables:[57]

- childhood economic conditions;

- childhood health;

- family distress (while still a child);

- current socioeconomic status; and

- current health.

---

57   Y. Kamiya, M. Doyle, J.C. Henretta & V. Timonen, 2013, 'Depressive symptoms among older adults: The impact of early and later life circumstances and marital status', *Aging & Mental Health*, vol. 17, no. 3, pp. 349–357.

Perhaps unsurprisingly to those of us who are acutely aware of the lifelong impact of major life events, the researchers found that, among men, 'growing up in a poor family, having had a parent with substance abuse problems and reporting poor childhood health have significant total effects on the level of depressive symptoms at old age'. Among women, 'growing up in a poor family or poor health in childhood has significant total effects on late-life depression'. The enduring impact of what happens to you as a child was emphasised in the study when the researchers controlled for current health and current socioeconomic status. So even when an individual's present-day health and financial circumstances are taken into account, 'those who had poor childhood health [still] have higher depressive symptoms'. It is indeed very much what happens to you that influences your life for a long, long time – no matter 'what you do about it'.

One example that's fun to debate is smoking. That a billion people around the world still smoke cigarettes, and that 5 million of them die each year from tobacco-related diseases, is staggering when you consider the enormous amount of freely available evidence that proves beyond any doubt whatsoever that it's a product designed to infect its purchaser with a terminal illness. So why can't people just quit smoking? The frequent debate often coalesces around smokers being too weak, too manipulated, too hedonic, too stressed, too fat, too unhappy, too insecure, too whatever.

What each of these factors dismisses too easily, as one study put it, are 'the causes of the causes'. In an analysis of more than 2000 British people from the time they were born until the time they were 66 years of age, the researchers concluded that 'childhood circumstances predicted adult smoking habits'. They go further. If a participant had a father who hailed from a blue-collar social class, that participant had a higher chance of being an adult smoker. If a participant had a mother who only managed to get a primary school education and nothing more, that participant similarly had a higher chance of being an adult smoker. The researchers conclude: 'This study highlights the major role of early life circumstances as causes of inequalities in health. It emphasises how important it is, in the context of the policy debate, to recognise the intergenerational transmission of risk and the accumulation of disadvantages that can occur during childhood.' Indeed, what their research clearly demonstrates is that what happens in one's childhood is 'almost as powerful' in determining the risk of mortality in adulthood as smoking itself, such that 'the effects of early life circumstances were seen to extend far into adult life'.[58]

That doesn't mean that what one does as an adult has no effect. Of course it does. But to pretend that your circumstances leading up to that point don't have an influence – and a significant one at that – is, well, to pretend.

Let's now look at another example of decisions in adulthood that are influenced significantly by life circumstances: the decision to become a sex worker. Now, a sanctimonious individual might assert that deciding to be a sex worker is a voluntary act, which means it's a perfect case of 'how you react', 'how you deal with it' and 'what you do about it'. But it's really not that straightforward, as more trusted information indicates.

One study was conducted in the Indian state of Nagaland, where thousands of women earn an income from sex work and where more than 16 per cent are infected with HIV. The researchers surveyed 200 of these women, and interviewed 30 more for greater depth of understanding. What they learned was that

---

58   I. Giesinger, P. Goldblatt, P. Howden-Chapman, M. Marmot, D. Kuh
     & E. Brunner, 2013, 'Association of socioeconomic position with
     smoking and mortality: the contribution of early life circumstances
     in the 1946 birth cohort', *Journal of Epidemiology and Community
     Health*, vol. 68, no. 1, pp. 275–279.

there are indeed life circumstances that compel these vulnerable people to make the decision to become a sex worker. Here are some statistics that illustrate the point. The largest proportion of sex workers were previously unemployed. The second largest were school dropouts. Likewise, a vast majority were living in insecure accommodation, such as a rental property, a friend's place or a pimp's house. More than half described their family relationship in unfavourable terms. In two-thirds of cases, their entry into sex work was unplanned, with the arrangements most often made by someone else and at a venue such as a hotel. And as for condom use – well, that was non-existent in the early days of their sex work. One of the participants describes it like this: 'There are some useless men who won't use condoms. It becomes difficult to negotiate with them because they threaten me, and so to avoid creating a problem I do it without using a condom.'[59]

It is easy but ignorant and insulting to suggest that these women have a choice. It's frequently their only option if they want to earn enough to feed their

59 K.J. Bowen, B. Dzuvichu, A.E. Devine, J. Hocking, M. Kermode, & R. Rungsung, 2011, 'Life circumstances of women entering sex work in Nagaland, India', *Asia-Pacific Journal of Public Health*, vol. 23, no. 6, pp. 843–851.

children and other relatives. That they were primary school dropouts or without gainful employment or afflicted by a form of homelessness is, to paraphrase an earlier study, a selection of the myriad 'causes of the causes', many of which are beyond an individual's immediate control.

Let's look at one final piece of research before bringing this series of pious quotations to a close. This one looked at the world of crime, and, more specifically, the factors that led people to embark into it. The researchers were intrigued by prior studies that found criminality among men was lower when they were employed, in the military or married. They wanted to expand on this empirical work by conducting a study that analysed criminals and non-criminals, males and females, from the age of 12 until the age of 72.

Before going further, it's important to distinguish between two schools of thought: the 'static theory' and the 'dynamic theory'. The static theory suggests that the extent to which an individual commits a criminal offence is due to his or her own propensity for crime. In other words, some people are inherently more inclined to be criminals, and nothing that happens in their life will change that. Conversely, the dynamic theory proposes that, sure, some people are more predisposed to criminality than others, but that other circumstances in their lives push them over the edge into criminal behaviour. So this study, in a sense, was a contest between static theory and dynamic theory.

The researchers analysed over 4600 individuals in the Netherlands who had committed serious crimes, such as robbery, violence, murder, rape, child molestation and drug offences. They included in their analysis another sample of Dutch folk, this time a thousand or so who had committed other types of crime, such as shoplifting, vandalism, fraud, theft and assault. The results reflected a robust defence of the dynamic theory, because 'static theories offer too simplified a view on development of crime over time'. Convictions, for example, among those whose crimes were of a milder variety, were far more prevalent among those who had been separated from their partner for a long period of time. More specifically, when an individual was married, that individual was 27 per cent less likely to be convicted of a crime. In contrast, those who were separated were 44 per cent more likely to be criminals, compared to when they were married. Even among the hardcore criminals, being divorced boosted the rate at which they offended by 13 per cent. 'Overall, these figures clearly show the substantial consequences of transitions in life circumstances, as predicted by dynamic theories,' the scholars concluded.[60]

That doesn't mean we excuse crime or forgive it. It just means we understand it better when we look at the 'causes of the causes'. That's only possible if we're not glibly uttering that what happens to an individual is unimportant. Manifestly, it's extremely important in determining the person they become and the decisions they eventually make.

Imagine, too, being the victim of those crimes. These are serious events that can alter the rest of one's life in ways that are inconceivable – too inconceivable to simplistically assume that an adjustment in attitude will enable recovery.

Ultimately, if what happens to someone in life can influence them for the better – such as a happy marriage, a lottery win, a good upbringing, a safe haven, a secure job – then surely the opposite can have a negative effect. So let's edit the citations that began this chapter, beginning with W. Mitchell's:

> **'It's not only what happens to you;**
> **it's also what you do about it – assuming**

---

60 A.A.J. Blokland & P. Nieuwbeerta, 2005, 'The effects of life circumstances on longitudinal trajectories of offending', *Criminology*, vol. 43, no. 4, pp. 1203–1240.

you haven't been too screwed up by what
happened to you.'

Something similar for Terry Riley:

'It's not only what happens to you in life that
matters; what matters is also how you deal
with it – assuming you have the physical and
mental capacity to actually deal with it.'

A mathematical adjustment for Chuck Swindoll:

'Life is mostly what happens to you
and partly how you react to it.'

And, finally, something a little simpler for Epictetus:

'It's not only what happens to you, but
also how you react to it that matters.'

14

'MANY HANDS MAKE LIGHT WORK'

—JOHN HEYWOOD

Many years ago, there lived a German psychology professor named Maximilien Ringelmann, who ran a curious experiment. He invited participants to pull a rope. The rope was attached to a machine that measured the strength of each individual's pull. As each of the participants pulled the rope, Professor Ringelmann would record the strength of the pull. He would then get the participants to pull the rope together. Now, one would reasonably expect the strength of the combined pull to equal the sum of their individual pulls. But that's not what happened. When pulling the rope together, the participants exerted significantly less effort. In groups of eight, for example, they were pulling the rope only half as strongly as they were when they were on their own. This discovery gave rise to what became known as the 'Ringelmann effect', which broke the stereotype that 'team participation leads to increased effort, that group morale and cohesiveness spur individual enthusiasm, that by pulling together groups can achieve any goal, that in unity there is strength'.[61]

Since then, the Ringelmann effect has come to be known instead as social loafing, which is the tendency people have to lessen the effort they invest when they're working on a task with others. That this phenomenon has been proven time and again calls into question the dictum of English writer John Heywood that many hands make light work. Sure, sometimes they do, but it's also just as frequently true that many hands often complicate the work, delaying it and frustrating it, as well as giving people the opportunity to absolve themselves of responsibility by means of the anonymity that comes from being one player among many.

So what drives social loafing? Three factors. First, a preference among many people to work individually.

61   B. Latane, K. Williams & S. Harkins, 1979, 'Many hands make light the work: The causes and consequences of social loafing', *Journal of Personality & Social Psychology*, vol. 37, no. 6, pp. 822–832.

Second, a group in which one or more members has little care for winning. And third, environments where people don't really need to rely on each other, and yet are still lumped together. There's probably no context more apt for studying this behaviour than a university setting, and the group assignments that lecturers set their students. Almost invariably, students detest these assessments. The star pupil hates having no choice but to take on most of the work, while the apathetic colleagues despise having to make time for meetings they have absolutely no interest in. Pretty much all round, these experiences are an anguish-ridden torture chamber – not unlike many workplaces.

It was in a study of 365 of these torture victims that the three factors were found to play a critical role. The students were surveyed and analysed multiple times over a four-month period, with the obvious finding that those who retch at the thought of group work – and who may be content with mediocre performance, and who can't see the point of working with others on tasks that don't seem interdependent – would subsequently put their feet up and just wait for the whole ordeal to be over.[62]

---

62   E.M. Stark, J.D. Shaw & M.K. Duffy, 2007, 'Preference for group work, winning orientation, and social loafing behavior in groups', *Group & Organization Management*, vol. 32, no. 6, pp. 699–723.

It's much like being on jury duty, which was the focus of another social loafing study. In this one, more than 100 people were asked to participate in a mock trial, in which they had to decide whether a deceased man had suicided (thereby finding in favour of the insurance company, which was the defendant) or whether the deceased had died accidentally while cleaning his hunting rifle (thereby finding in favour of his wife, who, as the plaintiff, stood to pocket a generous insurance payout). To help them reach a decision, the participants were provided with seven pages of information containing eight distinct pieces of information, including the deceased's mood at the time of his death, his financial status and his stated plans that day. The participants were required to read that information and to then recall it. Those who were told they were working individually had a significantly better recall rate than those who were told they were working in groups. 'The anticipation that a decision was to be made collectively led individuals to process information less effort-fully than participants who believed they were making an individual decision.'[63] You can

---

63   D.D. Henningsen, M.G. Cruz & M.L. Miller, 2000, 'Role of social loafing in predeliberation decision making', *Group Dynamics: Theory, Research, and Practice*, vol. 4, no. 2, pp. 168–175.

just imagine the impact this would have on real juries, where maximum cognitive effort should be demanded at all times.

This is about much more than juries and school students, though. It's about the working world as we know it. It's about the age of groupism. 'In recent years, the emphasis on groups and teams has gone far beyond any rational assessment of their practical usefulness. We are in the age of groupomania,' one group of researchers has written. 'Teams have become endowed with almost mystical qualities . . . Teams, it is implied, will cure almost any organizational disease, solve any problem, achieve any goal. But of course, they do not.'[64]

The scholars who authored this statement argue that teams only work when the individuals who constitute those teams are highly skilled, capable and driven – which are, of course, the very attributes required to perform well individually. Instead, organisations opt to make light work via the use of many hands, and so they overemphasise 'team processes, team cohesion, team

---

64   E.A. Locke, D. Tirnauer, Q. Roberson, B. Goldman, M.E. Latham & E. Weldon, 2001, 'The importance of the individual in an age of groupism', in M.E. Turner (ed.), *Groups at Work: Theory and research*, Lawrence Erlbaum, New Jersey, pp. 501–528.

identity and team performance at the expense of individual thinking, individual performance, individual identity, and individual motivation'. The consequence, which they document in dozens upon dozens of empirical studies, is a dysfunctional environment that prioritises an ideological frenzy for group work when, in many cases, the organisation can perform better by leaving individuals alone so they can just get on with their jobs.

The researchers focused on three types of social loafing in particular. One is the 'free rider', who benefits twice: once from the hard work of others, and then from the equal distribution of rewards. Free riders get away with it because the sheer size of teams these days enables them to remain anonymous. The second is the 'sucker effect', which describes those who are aware of the free riders in their team and, in a bid to avoid being taken for a ride, slacken off as well. The third is known as 'felt dispensability', which occurs when people reduce their effort when they feel as though they're not needed. If their teammates seem highly competent and capable, and it's not apparent how they themselves can add value, they often choose to instead take it easy rather than finding ways to be valuable.

Even if these three factors didn't exist, there's one other that definitely does: groupthink. The illusion of unanimous decisions screws up effective decision-making and isolates the outliers who disagree with the group's consensus. As the researchers conclude: 'Simply throwing a large number of minds (i.e., a team) at the problem will not necessarily produce effective results . . . Yes, we need to use some teams and groups in the management of organizations. But we should not forget that they are composed of individuals and that, at root, organizations rise and fall as a result of the thinking (or nonthinking) of individual minds.'

Are we talking here about exceptions? No, this appears to be the norm. In an exhaustive study of 33 teams across a wide range of fields, including sport, manufacturing, finance, management and others, only four teams were found to be working well. This surprised the professors, who were conducting the research in the hope that they would find what works. Instead, they discovered that the remaining 29 teams 'had problems so severe that [the] analysis was mainly about what had gone wrong with them'. One of the biggest reasons these teams and many others fail miserably is that managers impulsively create a team for work that is better performed by people alone. 'It is a mistake – a common one and often a fatal one – to use a team for work that requires the exercise of powers that reside within and are best expressed by individual human beings.'[65]

Yet team-based work continues unabated in organisations, most of which have romanticised the idea of group work. They've fallen so in love with the claims made 'in the popular press and quasi-scientific press about the effectiveness, and indeed superiority, of team-based work. In contrast to the somewhat messianic tone of some such claims, empirical data from both laboratory studies and organizational settings are much less impressive.' And the authors of that passage really know what they're talking about. They reviewed every credible study on teamwork, finding that there is unambiguously a mismatch between the enthusiasm managers have for teams and the performance those teams eventually generate – or, rather, don't generate. They call it the 'romance of teams', and define it as 'a faith in the effectiveness of team-based work that is not supported by, or is even consistent with, relevant empirical evidence.'[66]

---

65   J.R. Hackman, 1998, 'Why teams don't work', in R.S. Tindale, L. Heath, J. Edwards, E.J. Posavac, F.B. Bryant, Y. Suarez-Balcazar, E. Henderson-King & J. Myers (eds), *Theory & Research on Small Groups*, New York, Plenum Press, pp. 245–267.

66   N.J. Allen & T.D. Hecht, 2004, 'The "romance of teams": Toward an understanding of its psychological underpinnings and implications', *Journal of Occupational & Organizational Psychology*, vol. 77, no. 4, pp. 436–461.

In their extensive analysis, they uncovered myriad studies that demonstrate 'people believe teams are effective because they are unaware of evidence to the contrary'. For example, in contrast to the widespread perception that brainstorming activities lead to a greater number of good ideas, the converse is true. Groups actually come up with fewer ideas – or, if it's an especially fortunate day, the same number of ideas – when compared to individuals working alone. Their ideas are also frequently of lower quality than the loners' contributions. Some of the other findings include the following:

- Managers often establish teams without considering whether the organisational context necessitates it or the work itself demands it. This is usually motivated 'by a desire to give the organization an inclusive and consultative appearance. A consequence of having representatives from various organizational functions or departments who are not really required on the team means that some people belong to teams that hold little meaning for them.' There are frequently other consequences, too, such as the higher costs involved in managing teams and the difficulty of implementing adequate systems to support them.

- From the perspective of employees, these consequences can ramp up the pressure to conform to the idealised notion of what a team should be. Imagine being a candidate for a job where you bravely admit in the interview that you're not a team player. You'd probably have the interview terminated immediately. Instead, you'd be inclined to just be like everyone else – not only in the interview but on the job, too – and pretend to be an advocate of teams, when most of us know the truth deep down. 'Thus, some individuals may experience unnecessary and avoidable employee discomfort as a result of projecting false enthusiasm', the culmination of which is, in many cases, angst and social loafing.

If John Heywood were alive today, would he still think that 'many hands make light work'? I doubt it. He certainly wouldn't if he was at all familiar with the many studies that have been released suggesting otherwise. With the benefit of all that we now know, I imagine he would, sooner or later, have adapted his line to something like this:

'Many hands make light of the work.'

15

THE IMPOSSIBILITY OF ACHIEVING THE IMPOSSIBLE

t really is somewhat hilarious that we encourage achievement of the impossible when it's difficult enough for most of us even to achieve the possible. Whatever happened to baby steps? So when Napoleon Bonaparte says, **'Impossible is a word only to be found in the dictionary of fools,'** he'd better call me a fool, because the realistically achievable should surely be the priority. When newspaperman Doug Larson says that **'some of the world's greatest feats were accomplished by people not smart enough to know they were impossible'**, well, maybe that's because they weren't actually impossible. The sublime Audrey Hepburn once said: **'Nothing is impossible; the word**

itself says "I'm possible". The second half of her quotation may be semantically true, but life is full of limitations. It is impossible to count to infinity, to fly unaided, to grow a tail, to travel back in time, to live forever, to walk on water, to uncrack an egg, to drink boiling water. Humans themselves are full of limitations – thereby rendering jack-of-all-trades Les Brown also entirely incorrect when he says, **'Life has no limitations except the ones you make.'**

This emphasis on the impossible gives rise to something known as 'unrealistic optimism' – the technical term describing those who are, funnily enough, unrealistically optimistic. So, you might think, what's the harm in that? A lot. The empirical literature is replete with studies demonstrating the damage that ensues. You can see it in unrealistically optimistic smokers who think they won't be part of the 67 per cent who die from smoking-related illnesses. You can see it in unrealistic optimists who get married despite the startling statistic that one in two marriages ends in divorce. You can see it among those unrealistically optimistic bankers during the Global Financial Crisis who held the warped belief that their dubious actions wouldn't have catastrophic consequences. You can see it among those who practice unsafe sex in the mistaken belief they won't pick up an STI. You can see it in those who think they'll be fine in retirement until they retire and realise they haven't saved enough. You can see it in unrealistically optimistic entrepreneurs who establish start-up businesses that, in a majority of cases, end in failure within the first few years, losing not just the enterprises but also, often, their livelihoods.

The problem is that 'most people believe they are more capable than average and that their chances of a better future are higher than those of others'.[67] Those with this self-serving bias are the ripest targets of the aim-for-impossibility advocates. These are the people who perceive themselves as being a cut above the rest of us, so that any talk of achieving the impossible makes them think, 'Hell, yeah! If anyone can do it, it's me!'

This is not a matter of self-esteem. Self-esteem is something everyone should acquire. This is about much more than self-esteem. It's about a future goal – one that is by definition unattainable, but in which an individual nonetheless inordinately invests. The entrepreneurial example mentioned above is a prime illustration. In such situations, a pessimistic entrepreneur is better placed to recognise when to shut a failing business. An unrealistically optimistic entrepreneur is more likely to persevere,

---

67   M. Coelho, 2010, 'Unrealistic optimism: still a neglected trait', *Journal of Business and Psychology*, vol. 25, no. 3, pp. 397–408.

only closing the business once the losses have become debilitating. An extensive analysis of empirical studies on this topic, the conclusions of which were quoted briefly in the preceding paragraph, found that 'even if optimism leads entrepreneurs to work harder and to be happier, it is their unrealistic beliefs which may be quite damaging. They will tend to overestimate chances of success and therefore choose the wrong business strategies, will back strategies that depend on skills they do not possess (as opposed to relying on the expertise of outsiders), and will concentrate on positive feedback and ignore negative feedback – however important it might be.'

In the same way that a profound sense of self-belief inflates one's unrealistic optimism, so too does a sense of power. 'It is this intoxicating effect of power that is a particular engine of overconfidence' and that leads to a number of consequences, such as the risk-taking that personifies those obsessed with achieving the seemingly impossible. Why? Because overconfidence has been found in empirical research to be 'one of the most prevalent and most catastrophic impediments to judgment and decision making'. This is a corollary not only of a swollen perception of ability but also of knowledge, of action, of thought, of rightness. 'As a result, these individuals are more likely to anchor their own private information without considering cues present in

the environment or alternate perspectives of others'[68] –
with such cues and perspectives being those shrieking
that there is indeed such a thing as The Impossible and
that they had better stop now before they discover in
the crudest of ways that it exists.

The authors of the quotations in the last paragraph
ran one experiment in particular that was quite telling.
The participants were required to take part in a mock
negotiation. The dispute was between a condominium
developer and a carpentry contractor, with the former
claiming thousands of dollars of undue monies from
the latter. The participants were required to play each
role. Prior to starting, though, they were asked a pertinent question: 'How confident are you that you will
reach a favorable outcome for yourself?'

Guess what? Those who were more confident performed worse than those who were less confident. As
a consequence, they were required to pay a fine that
was greater than it would have been if they'd held more
modest expectations of their own success. Ironically,
the sense of power that fed their ballooning overconfidence was the same power that ended up diminished as
a result of their poor performance in the task.

---

68   N. Sivanathan & A.D. Galinsky, 2007, 'Power and overconfidence',
     IACM 2007 Meetings Paper, http://dx.doi.org/10.2139/ssrn.1100725.

This connection between overconfidence, a bias for optimism and adverse performance was found in another study, except this one moved beyond an experiment and into the real world – or as real as the stock market gets, anyway. These researchers analysed firms on the American exchange that had misreported their earnings, comparing them to firms that had not. Consistent with prior research, the scholars found a much greater prevalence of optimism and overconfidence among the misreporting executives. It was, however, unintentional. They overstated their future earnings simply from a belief that the impossible was possible. Until they discovered that they had erred. And it's what happens next that is most pertinent. On learning that they were going to miss their targets, these executives went on to intentionally misreport their earnings, thereby earning themselves a civil lawsuit from the federal regulator. Their unintentional act, triggered by optimism bias and overconfidence, led to an intentional act of misconduct. They had effectively become fraudsters.[69]

A likeminded analysis also looked at executives' optimism and overconfidence, but this time in relation

---

69   C.M. Schrand & S.L.C. Zechman, 2012, 'Executive overconfidence and the slippery slope to financial misreporting', *Journal of Accounting and Economics*, vol. 53, no. 1–2, pp. 311–329.

to the impact on the firms' share price. More than 20,000 pieces of firm-related data were analysed. In sum, overconfident CEOs were significantly more likely to lead their firms to a share price crash. Why? Because they're more inclined to continue with pet projects that are clearly not working; they have a greater tendency to ignore negative feedback from wise stake-holders; and they're more likely to conceal bad news in the hope that their misguided optimism will bear fruit.[70] This research follows earlier studies demonstrating that overconfident CEOs are also more likely to drive their firms to embark on value-destroying mergers, to inefficiently utilise limited investment opportunities, and to take on substantially more debt. They're not mean-spirited. They're not intentionally deceitful. They're genuinely doing what they think is best for their organisation. It's just that they have an inflated sense of belief in themselves and their favoured projects. They're chasing the impossible, in the face of mounting evidence which they've been ignoring and hiding, and when they finally realise it is indeed impossible, it's too late.

---

70   J.B. Kim, Z. Wang & L. Zhang, 2016, 'CEO overconfidence and stock price crash risk', *Contemporary Accounting Research*, vol. 33, no. 4, pp. 1720–1749.

There's another issue worth noting about the so-called impossible, and that's something known as 'asymmetric information'. From a social science perspective, it's a term that describes the gap between an individual's overconfidence and their actual competence. To put it another way, it's the gap between the possible and the impossible, with many people coerced into chasing the latter in a bitter example of asymmetry in action. And it seems to affect the poor performers the most. University students in one experiment completed three tests and were asked afterwards to predict their mark. Most of those who performed the worst actually thought they had performed quite well. By contrast, those who were the best performers were more likely to be less confident of their performance, and to more accurately predict their mark. Even when the poor performers received negative feedback after the first disappointing test and then the second, they were still more likely to overconfidently predict their performance in the third.[71]

After running several experiments across different cohorts, the scholars concluded: 'The great philosophies and religions, and many of the great works of literature,

---

71   P.J. Ferraro, 2010, 'Know thyself: Incompetence and overconfidence', *Atlantic Economic Journal*, vol. 38, no. 2, pp. 183–196.

describe the dangers of overconfidence, the honor of humility, and the necessity of self-introspection that leads to knowing oneself. Given the link between competence and self-awareness, however, it is not surprising that more than a millennium of efforts to develop social norms to constrain overconfidence has done little to solve the problem of overconfidence. In a way, the problem is unsolvable: the less one knows, the less one is able to know that he does not know . . . Modern social norms in Western, industrialized nations seem, in fact, to encourage overconfidence.'

And no individuals are guiltier at perpetuating that overconfidence than those with which this chapter is concerned. Let's revise, then, their quotations, starting with Napoleon:

'Impossible is a word invariably found in the Cambridge, Oxford, Macquarie and Merriam-Webster dictionaries, among many others.'

Doug Larson:

'Some of the world's greatest feats were accomplished by people smart enough to know they were possible.'

Audrey Hepburn:

> **'Much is impossible. Deal with it.'**

Les Brown:

> **'Life has many limitations,**
> **including the ones you make'.**

16

'THAT WHICH DOES NOT KILL US MAKES US STRONGER'

—FRIEDRICH NIETZSCHE

Far be it from me to criticise the philosopher and supreme intellect Friedrich Nietzsche, so of course I won't. Much like all the others mentioned in this book, he's deserving of admiration. But this one quotation – these nine comforting words – have remarkably stood the test of time since they were first penned in the late 1800s. But how true are they? Are we really strengthened by that which does not destroy us? Sometimes, yes. Oftentimes, not. Indeed, 'despite the familiarity of the adage that whatever does not kill us makes us stronger, the preponderance of empirical evidence seems to offer little support for it'.

Now, I have to declare a bias. I have not sought to offer a balanced view in this book. Neither have I sought to provide the most comprehensive scholarly analysis of each motivational position. I've merely sought to poke holes through perceived truisms that don't deserve to be considered truisms; at least, not in the absolutist terms in which they're commonly framed. But the authors of the statement that ended the preceding paragraph certainly did seek a balanced perspective. They genuinely wanted to find out whether that which doesn't kill us does indeed make us stronger, so they looked at a construct referred to as 'cumulative adversity', which is when people are confronted repeatedly by a number of negative events. The scholars surveyed roughly 2000 people five times over a period of two years in order to track not only the adversities by which they were burdened but also the impact these had on their levels of long-term distress, life (dis)satisfaction, functional impairment and stress.

Unsurprisingly, the researchers found that the more individuals experience cumulative adversity, the greater their subsequent levels of distress, dissatisfaction with life, functional impairment and post-traumatic stress. But here's the most curious finding of all: 'People with *low* lifetime adversity reported *better* outcomes over time than did people who had experienced *no* adversity.[72] That means there is some truth to the saying that whatever doesn't kill you makes you stronger – but only if what almost killed you is moderate in its impact. Should it be severe, which one can safely assume is usually the case in a near-miss metaphorical homicide, well, grave consequences almost certainly ensue even if you've been spared the grave.

Let's look at one adverse event in particular: job loss. Many studies have already demonstrated the mental health implications of being fired. That's because the involuntary loss of one's job damages a person's self-esteem, since our identity, relationships, status, finances, skill utilisation and more are often attached to the work we all perform. One argument, though, could be that those consequences are short-term. Once they subside, the sacked employee might look back and realise how much better they are now, how much they've learned, how much they've grown. Or not. In research much like the one noted above, more than 600 employees whose employment was recently terminated were

---

72   M.D. Seery, E.A. Holman & R.C. Silver, 2010, 'Whatever does not kill us: Cumulative lifetime adversity, vulnerability, and resilience', *Journal of Personality and Social Psychology*, vol. 99, no. 6, pp. 1025–1041.

tracked for a period of two years so that the scholars could assess the physical and mental impact of their situation. What they discovered was that being sacked and the ensuing period of unemployment and financial strain resulted in higher rates of depression, which can subsequently trigger a sense that one has lost control, thereby further eroding physical and mental health.

Now, here's what makes that study especially interesting. It's not just that those consequences remained stable for at least two years. It's also the simple fact that job loss is, in many respects, reversible. It's possible to be hired somewhere else in some capacity. And yet, despite the potential reversibility of unemployment, the physical and psychological scars remain. A downward spiral can also begin. For many participants, the depression that emerged following the termination of their employment debilitated them such that their chances for re-employment were hindered.[73]

So that's what happens when it's a one-off event that could, theoretically at least, still give its victims a

---

73 R.H. Price, J.N. Choi & A.D. Vinokur, 2002, 'Links in the chain of adversity following job loss: How financial strain and loss of personal control lead to depression, impaired functioning, and poor health', *Journal of Occupational Health Psychology*, vol. 7, no. 4, pp. 302–312.

glimmer of hope. You can probably imagine the enduring impact when that which does not kill us is not an event but a condition – such as a chronic disease – whereby 'the cumulative burden of adversity interferes with overall coping'. This burden of adversity can be something as mild as anxiety, which in itself is far from a mild psychological state, to post-traumatic stress disorder, which can be debilitating.

As an example, let's look at a heart attack. The medical episode itself is not the only adverse event. The cumulative burden that then follows includes the new nutrition regimen to which the patient must adhere; the unexpected complications that materialise; the ongoing physical pain; the impact on one's social life; the impact on one's self-esteem; the risk it could all happen again; the ongoing medical tests; the process of rehabilitation; the undesired changes to one's lifestyle; the funding of medical bills; and so on. It's no wonder that many studies have found that a heart attack that hasn't killed someone hasn't necessarily made them stronger. If anything, it's made them weaker, as depression and PTSD frequently set in. Patients' capacity to cope is often diminished. This may 'explain why individuals frequently fall short of meeting clinician expectations regarding adherence to medical regimens, especially timely care seeking . . . especially when cumulative adversity may promote avoidance . . . and distort perception'.[74]

Let's look at one final example, this time from childhood. If Nietzsche's idea is correct, then traumas that children suffer should strengthen rather than weaken them, especially as they enter adulthood and reflect on what they have endured. Right? You and I both know the answer, so feel free to skip the next paragraph.

Okay, you're still with me. I'll keep it short. A survey of almost 11,000 adults enquired as to the participants' history of childhood physical abuse, sexual abuse, emotional abuse, physical neglect and emotional neglect. Those who had been the victims of such crimes were found to be significantly more likely to grow up as adults who were less stable, more sensitive, more anxious and angrier, and who had greater difficulty coping with the vicissitudes of life. These individuals were labelled not stronger but 'maladaptive'. The only exception was in relation to physical maltreatment, which appears to not be as harmful in the long term as emotional and sexual abuse – in which case, as the scholars note, 'what does

74   A.A. Alonzo, 2000, 'The experience of chronic illness and post-traumatic stress disorder: the consequences of cumulative adversity', *Social Science & Medicine*, vol. 50, no. 10, pp. 1475–1484.

not kill me makes me weaker'.[75]

Nietzsche can be forgiven. Almost all the research disproving his theory was conducted after his death. Still, his quotation can't avoid a much-needed edit:

'That which does not kill us usually makes us weaker, and only occasionally stronger.'

75   R. Sudbrack, P.H. Manfro, I.M. Kuhn, H.W. de Carvalho & D.R. Lara, 2015, 'What doesn't kill you makes you stronger and weaker: How childhood trauma relates to temperament traits', *Journal of Psychiatric Research*, vol. 62, no. 1, pp. 123–129.

17

THE DIRTY BUSINESS
OF BUSYNESS

'm not exaggerating when I say I work in excess
of 90 hours a week. So when I come across art-
ist and educator Robert Henri's exhortation to
'do whatever you do intensely', I immediately
think, 'Hell, yeah!' Likewise, when Thomas Jefferson's
quotation – **'determine never to be idle'** – appears
on my radar, I'm instantly encouraged and reassured,
especially when the rest of it is included: **'No person
will have occasion to complain of the want of time
who never loses any. It is wonderful how much
may be done if we are always doing.'** And when
there's confusion over who said what between actress
Lucille Ball (**'The more things you do, the more you**

can do') and essayist William Hazlitt (**'The more we do, the more we can do'**), I really don't care. What matters is that they're affirming the extreme lifestyle I've adopted. Even though research indicates it's unwise.

One relevant piece of research was an ethnographic study in which professors spent 2400 hours observing families as they went about their day. They shadowed them as they worked. They shadowed them at school. They shadowed them while they were having dinner, attended meetings, did their homework, watched TV, played video games, ran errands, did the shopping, went to parties, attended church, performed household chores. They would often spend between 12 and 14 hours with them each day, for days at a time, over a period of up to four months. They then maintained contact with them for up to another eight months. It was an exhaustive series of observations, but it was momentous fieldwork that generated findings that truly reflected the nature of busyness. Those findings were characterised by the role of technology.

Technology, once upon a time, was supposed to free us. It was supposed to give us more time. It's had the opposite effect. Actually, it's made us busier: it's given us more things to do, more things to stay on top of, more ways of staying in contact, and more ways of remaining plugged in to work and tasks and responsibilities.

It was therefore common among the families in the study to be ridiculously busy not only because of the daily constraints of time and space, but also because of technology's unique ability to compel people to do more, to squeeze more in. And it's not just technology's culpability. Consumerism is to blame here too. In their insatiable appetite for buying the latest and the best, many of the families had to work harder and longer just to catch up. The consequence is best summed up by one of the participants, who said, 'I don't live life, I manage it.'[76]

The scholars conclude by saying that 'regardless of whether people are working harder, they are working differently, with consequences for the everyday lives of individuals and social institutions. Indeed, an implication is that management activities may come to constitute everyday life, and mastery of tools and practices may come to define the good person and life. Discourses of productivity and efficiency, so familiar in the workplace, are imported into new spheres of life such as home and family.' Whether that's a good thing or a bad thing is for you to decide, but there is something overly clinical, is there not, in applying corporate management principles in the family home?

---

76   C.N. Darrah, 2007, 'The anthropology of busyness', *Human Organization*, vol. 66, no. 3, pp. 261–269.

And yet that clinical approach is destined to remain, since people have generally 'internalized the cultural norm of busyness, seeing being busy an important part of their identities'. That process of internalisation is evident in the simple fact that a busy lifestyle is a sign of a life that prioritises work ethic, efficiency, productivity and action – you know, all of what is espoused by Robert Henri, Thomas Jefferson, Lucille Ball and William Hazlitt. We've reached the point where people, when asked how they're doing, will almost invariably respond with 'busy'. It's not just an adjective; it's a badge of honour. It's not just a label; it's an identity. 'The value of busyness is so ingrained in work and leisure that for many it is hard to imagine a life that is not busy.' That was the conclusion of another field study, which found that busyness is seen by people as a personal value – they find it rewarding, fulfilling and meaningful – as well as a social norm, whereby cramming as much as possible into each day is just what everyone does these days, such that 'even when engaged in fun or leisure activities, [the] participants seemed task-oriented'.[77]

---

77 G. Leshed & P. Sengers, 2011, '"I lie to myself that I have freedom in my own schedule": productivity tools and experiences of busyness', *Proceedings of the SIGCHI Conference on Human Factors in Computing Systems, Vancouver, 7–12 May*, pp. 905–914.

As a result, their lives are characterised by endless doing rather than just being, the consequence of which is a level of anxiety associated with not keeping up, as well as a deep longing for relaxation and downtime, which many do not allow themselves. The guilt derived from simply doing nothing has even led to the development of a widely used term – 'recharging the batteries' – lest others think this temporary period of idleness is permanent. Other implications of this study include that individuals used a range of technologies and devices to help them be more productive in the hope it would give them a sense of control. Ironically, the opposite occurred. The more they depended on these tools, the less control they felt they had. They were indeed being controlled by deadlines and priorities, by meetings and appointments, by traffic and chores. That overwhelm, too, led to a range of conflicts between what these individuals really wanted to be doing with their time and what they found themselves having to prioritise instead. They might have loved being busy – and most of them certainly did – but it came at a price. That price was stress and tension.

It's a price that's seemingly paid for dearly in the West, especially in countries like the United States and Australia, where a declaration of busyness has become 'a type of bragging, as in "Look how important I am".

This would seem exceedingly curious to visitors from many other cultures – like bragging that you are having a nervous breakdown. It is readily accepted, however, in a culture that assumes time is money and that every moment not doing something is a wasted one. To be busy is to be a worthwhile person.'[78]

The analysis conducted by the scholar who made that last statement is fascinating because his investigation indicates that how a specific culture views busyness is quite revealing of its values. For example: 'How much and often should people work? What is the appropriate balance between work and play? Is speed a good thing? Should it be work before play or the other way around? Is there such a thing as doing nothing? Can time be wasted?' In cultures where the answers to those questions are: (i) a lot; (ii) what balance?; (iii) yes; (iv) the former; (v) no; and (vi) definitely, it's not unusual for busyness to serve as a psychological need and a 'compulsive activity that protects one from facing an existential void. By continuously focusing outward, a person may avoid facing him or herself. This type of busyness, in a sense, shuts down consciousness. It removes an individual from awareness of the present moment.'

78   R. Levine, 2005, 'A geography of busyness', *Social Research*, vol. 72, no. 2, pp. 355–370.

That is why mindfulness – such as stillness, intentional breathing, and meditation – is becoming more popular as an area of research, and as a growing practice, even within organisations. It reflects the consciousness, the awareness and the presence that seem to be lacking in our busy-obsessed world, a world that, by and large, is still oblivious to 'the infidelity of busyness'. This term was coined by a prolific researcher whose voluminous work has demonstrated that even though we fundamentally know we're living unsustainable lives and that we must slow down, we remain addicted to activity. We're still hooked on doing, on cramming, on not missing out, thereby engaging in infidelity 'or the fiction that we can balance it all, when all the facts keep telling us that the costs are outweighing the benefits'.[79]

So what are the benefits of mindfulness? Or, to put it another way, what are the benefits of non-busyness? Well, one of the most widely respected publications on the topic, which comprised a series of empirical studies, found significant positive effects on psychological well-being, less cognitive and emotional disturbance, greater

79   J. Kabat-Zinn, 2005, *Coming to Our Senses: Healing ourselves and the world through mindfulness*, Hyperion, New York.

self-regulation, less stress and fewer bad moods.[80]

Let's revisit the quotations that began this chapter, then, and amend them accordingly, starting with Robert Henri:

> **'Do whatever you do intensely.**
> **Then take a break.'**

Thomas Jefferson:

> **'Determine to be idle. It is wonderful**
> **how much we learn about ourselves when**
> **we are no longer always doing.'**

Lucille Ball:

> **'The more things you do, the more**
> **stress you accumulate.'**

William Hazlitt:

> **'The more we don't, the more we can be.'**

---

80   K.W. Brown & R.M. Ryan, 2003, 'The benefits of being present: mindfulness and its role in psychological well-being', *Journal of Personality and Social Psychology*, vol. 84, no. 4, pp. 822–848.

18

'IT'S BETTER TO BE
A LION FOR A DAY THAN
A SHEEP ALL YOUR LIFE'

–ELIZABETH KENNY

E lizabeth Kenny was an Australian nurse. Actually, she lacked nursing qualifications, yet she still managed to serve her country as a staff nurse during World War I. Afterwards, she opened her own backyard clinic, pioneered treatments that were ridiculed – and then widely adopted – by the medical fraternity, and developed training programs for doctors around the world. So to say that Sister Kenny was a lion rather than a sheep would be a fair statement. The problem with this quotation, though, is the denigration of sheep. We've come to a point in our modern society where leadership is glorified while followership is frowned upon, although no one acknowledges that we need less of the former and more of the latter, since leaders can't possibly lead without people who will follow them. There is nothing to be ashamed of in being a follower. There is an art to it; a science to it, even. And the more we worship leadership – the more we lionise it – the more we encourage people to pursue careers as leaders even when they're fundamentally not up to the task. They end up pursuing leadership for reasons of power, status, money – all the wrong reasons, really. If only we had valued the sheep as much as the lion, we wouldn't have as many ill-equipped leaders roaring and goring their way up the corporate ladder, ravenously seeking prey.

Here's a more scholarly exposition of this idea: 'Now, though, it's time, it's past time, to face facts . . . People without obvious sources of power, authority, and influence are far more consequential than we generally assume, and they are ubiquitous. To give them short shrift is to shortchange our understanding of both leaders and followers. In fact, as the result of changes now converging, followers are more important than ever before. And leaders nearly everywhere are more vulnerable to forces beyond their control, including those from the bottom up . . . The days when people in high places can sit pretty and do what they want how they want are over . . . Followers the world over are getting bolder and more strategic. They are less likely now than they were in the past to "know their place", to do as they are told, and to keep their opinions to themselves. This change, this small but potentially seismic shift in the balance of power between leaders and followers, constitutes a caution: leaders who ignore or dismiss their followers do so at their peril."[81]

The Harvard-based author of that passage has chronicled throughout history the ways in which followers exert enormous influence. The impact of the trade union movement over decades is one example. But even now, a time when the power of unions has diminished, what have since emerged are greater whistleblower protections; employee ownership schemes; affirmative action; the war for talent; shared leadership; shareholder activism; social media exposure; staff advocacy; the prioritisation of employee empowerment, engagement, involvement and job satisfaction; the human resources department; and employees with extensive knowledge and information (thanks to the World Wide Web and historically high levels of education) that, in many cases, surpass the traditionalist power of their employers. All of that is reason enough to immediately render followers no longer inferior.

---

81   B. Kellerman, 2008, *Followership: How followers are creating change and changing leaders*, Harvard Business Press, Boston.

Of course, there are many followers who are inferior. They're the ones who enable bad leadership to happen by not speaking out, by idolising, by being apathetic. They're the ones who politicise and scheme, manipulate and underperform, procrastinate and sabotage. But you'll find those characteristics among leaders, too. Especially among leaders. The majority of followers are the opposite. They might not all be superstars, but a fair chunk of them are good enough. And without these good-enough folk, our organisations and charities, our public service and diplomacy channels, our school canteens and volunteer committees, and myriad other fundamental functions of society just wouldn't function.

This is also why scholars reasonably assume that strong, capable, decent followers have a vital role to play beyond merely following. 'Leaders are not isolated actors immune from the influence of their followers.' In fact, followers are 'an integral part of leadership' because they can influence leaders to be better leaders via their skills of persuasion, the power they hold within the team, the relational proximity they have with their leader, the frequency of their interactions, and the knowledge and information they possess.'[82]

82   B. Oc & M.R. Bashshur, 2013, 'Followership, leadership and social influence', *The Leadership Quarterly*, vol. 24, no. 6, pp. 919–934.

And we shouldn't ignore the fact that everyone, really, is a follower. Everyone, despite their position on a hierarchy, despite the strength of their roar, still emits a bleat every now and again. After all, 'most individuals, even those with the highest levels of leadership responsibilities, answer to someone, be it the members of a board, the shareholders of a company, or the voters in an election'. And that's what's been found to be empirically true. In a study of military cadets, researchers compared the traits of leaders with the traits of followers, and found that 'the behaviors exhibited by the exemplary follower may not be that far off from those displayed by the effective leader'. Specifically, there are significant correlations between the leadership styles of dynamism and the followership style of active engagement, and between the leadership style of achievement orientation and the followership style of independent thinking. In other words, the lion with which leaders are most commonly associated is just as present in followers. Both leaders and followers can be 'the same animal with different spots'.[83]

The problem, though, is that the two animals are usually treated differently, and that's because of the

---

83   G.F. Tanoff & C.B. Barlow, 2002, 'Leadership and followership: Same animal, different spots?', *Consulting Psychology Journal: Practice and Research*, vol. 54, no. 3, pp. 157–165.

label attached to the term 'follower'. Labels are sticky. They're like a sticker on a purchased item that can't be removed, no matter how hard one tries to scratch it off. Even when most of the label is removed, the remnants are still there: the glue, the frayed paper. It's why prior research has revealed that labels can reinforce the negative connotations with which that label is regarded. One example is the label 'convicted felon'; another is 'drug addict'. Studies have shown that recidivism and addiction can be higher among those who are labelled as such; it's much like a self-fulfilling prophecy.

A trio of researchers who were intrigued by these findings sought to learn whether a similar principle applies in relation to followership. They ran two studies. The first was an experiment comprising approximately 150 participants. A third were told they were leaders, a third were followers, and a third weren't given a label at all. Those who were classified as followers had 'significantly lower positive affect'. 'Positive affect' is the psychological term that describes those who feel joyful, enthusiastic, confident and energetic. As a result, the followers in the experiment were much less likely to be proactive or to perform duties beyond their core role. In the second study, the researchers moved out of the laboratory and into the real world, with an analysis of almost 350 employees. The findings were replicated.

'Negative followership connotations persist because of the subordination of followership and the romance of leadership,' they concluded. In addition, to be a follower 'is associated with pejorative connotations . . . [and] compromises individuals' positive moods, and thus, discourages their active behaviors like helping others and taking initiative. Consequently, not only might followers be burdened by their label and position, but organizations might also suffer from their lack of motivation and uninspiring performance.'[84]

Basically, the value that followers can add and the ways in which they can influence and advocate and inform are diminished by how pervasively we glorify the lion and denigrate the sheep. But even the analogy itself is flawed. To be a lion-like leader is to be autocratic and dictatorial, which has been empirically found to be destabilising and to result in staff turnover, burnout, weaker relationships, lower productivity, lower employee satisfaction and many other adverse consequences. Conversely, to be a sheep-like leader is more closely related to the style of servant leadership, which many studies have found can generate greater

---

84 C. Hoption, A. Christie & J. Barling, 2012, 'Submitting to the follower label: Followership, positive affect, and extra-role behaviors', *Zeitschrift für Psychologie*, vol. 220, no. 4, pp. 221–230.

levels of trust, fairness, sustainability, employee commitment, proactive behaviour, creativity, helpfulness and collegiality.

Elizabeth Kenny's quotation most certainly is flawed, not only in its instructive merit but also in its metaphorical implication. So let's change it. Thankfully, we have a couple of options to play with:

'It's better to be a lion and a sheep.'

'It's not necessarily better to be a lion than a sheep.'

Dr James Adonis is one of Australia's most well-known team leadership educators, with a PhD that discovered the ways in which leaders can engage employees during organisational crises and significant change. His academic history is supported by practical experience in a variety of industries, and today he is still employed full-time in a leadership capacity with responsibility for more than 100 staff and significant long-term strategic projects.

James is a weekly business columnist with the Fairfax group of online news publications, such as the *Sydney Morning Herald* and the *Age*, and has been a professional speaker for more than a decade, helping hundreds of organisations around the world to successfully lead change and engage their employees.

jamesadonis.com
Twitter: @jamesadonis